A Scottish
Tradition

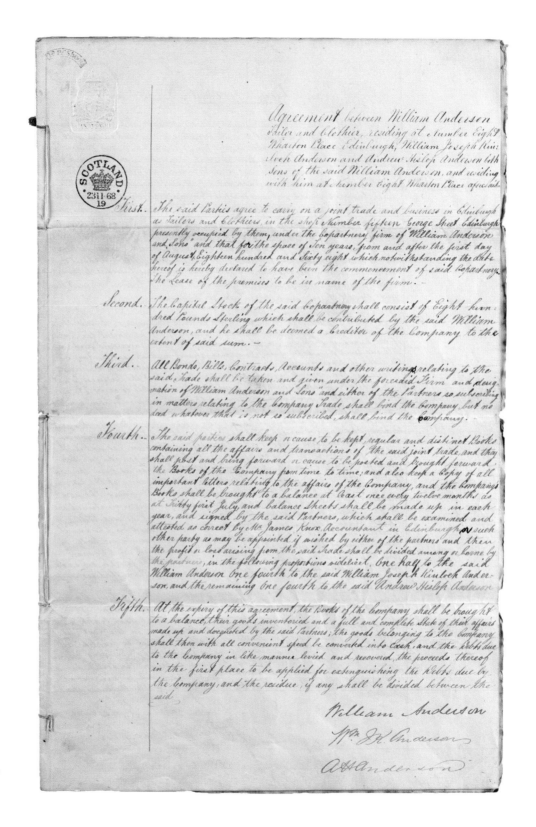

Right:
The original Partnership Agreement.
After many years gaining experience as a
tailor's cutter, William Anderson, in 1868,
founded his own business in partnership
with his two sons. It was situated at 15
George Street, Edinburgh, today the site
of the George Hotel, before moving to
number 17 and then across the street to
14 - 16 George Street where the company
was based for nearly a century.

Kinloch Anderson
SCOTLAND

*A Scottish
Tradition*

*Tailors
and Kiltmakers,
Tartan and
Highland Dress
since 1868*

Deirdre Kinloch Anderson

KINLOCH ANDERSON SCOTLAND – A SCOTTISH TRADITION

First published 2013 by Neil Wilson Publishing Ltd,
226 King Street, Castle Douglas, Scotland DG7 1DS,
in association with Kinloch Anderson Ltd, 4 Dock Street,
Leith, Edinburgh, Scotland, EH6 6EY

http://www.nwp.co.uk

http://www.kinlochanderson.com

An Incident in The Rebellion of 1745, by David Morier, is supplied by Royal
Collection Trust / © HM Queen Elizabeth II 2012

Lord Mungo Murray, 1668-1700, by John Michael Wright, is supplied by / ©
National Galleries Of Scotland, 2013

The Landing Of George IV at Leith 15th August 1822, by Alexander Carse, is
© and used by courtesy of Leith Police Station.

George IV In Highland Dress, by Sir David Wilkie, 1762-1830 is supplied by
Royal Collection Trust / © HM Queen Elizabeth II 2012

The photograph Balmoral Castle, is Copyright © 2013 J. Thomas,
and licensed under the Creative Commons Attribution Share alike 2.0
generic licence.

Design and layout by George Nicol, George Nicol Graphics Ltd, Edinburgh

The author and publisher have made every effort to ensure that the
information in this book was correct at time of press and that appropriate
rights and permissions to reproduce photographs and images have been
sought. The author and publisher do not assume and hereby disclaim any
liability to any party for any loss, damage, or disruption caused by errors or
omissions, whether such errors or omissions result from negligence,
accident, or any other cause.

ISBN: 978-1-90600067-7

Printed and bound in the EU

Contents

7   Foreword

9   Preface

10   Kinloch Anderson Timeline

15   The Historic Journey of Highland Dress

31   Uniforms for the Services

43   The Heritage Story of Kinloch Anderson

55   Highland Dress in Modern Times

69   Making the Kilt

75   Scottish Dress for Ladies

83   Early Marketing, Exporting and
     Brand Development

99   The Global Impact of Tartan

119 The Kinloch Anderson Heritage Room

This book would not have been achievable without the creative talent of George Nicol of George Nicol Graphics, the publishing guidance of Ron Grosset, Waverley Books, the photographic expertise of John McKenzie and the constant support of my Personal Assistant, Frances McLay.

I am also indebted to my husband, Douglas, for his sound advice, to my son John, for his valuable opinions and encouragement and to Eric Kinloch Anderson for his helpful suggestions regarding the text.

Foreword

At the beginning of the nineteenth century tartan was worn in the wild and unruly Highlands of Scotland, but hardly at all by civilized lowland Scots and never by Englishmen or foreigners. Yet within twenty years everything had changed. The world-famous, best-selling poems and novels of Walter Scott along with the Royal Visit of George IV to Edinburgh which Scott arranged and during which the King wore Highland Dress, converted tartan into the universally recognized symbol of Scotland.

It is largely because of tartan that our family firm celebrates a long history going back to 1868. Family businesses and tailoring businesses come and go, but Kinloch Anderson has survived and thrived into its sixth generation because of its unique reputation as Scotland's tartan and Highland Dress specialists. Neither Walter Scott nor my great-grandfather, who moved the Company from bespoke tailoring towards Highland Dress, could have guessed that tartan would become so fashionable all over the world. In the twenty-first century it is almost as popular in China and Japan as on its native heath and new tartans are designed and registered every year.

Although she is too modest to make the claim herself, the official Scottish Register of Tartans set up by the Scottish Parliament owed much to the advocacy and detailed hard work of Deirdre Kinloch Anderson, the author of this book.

Eric Kinloch Anderson

Sir Eric Kinloch Anderson, FRSE, KT, formerly Headmaster and Provost of Eton College and an authority on Sir Walter Scott, is a great-great-grandson of the Founder.

Six Generations of the Kinloch Anderson family

THE FOUNDER

William Anderson

SECOND GENERATION
Sons of the Founder

W Joseph Kinloch Anderson

A Hislop Anderson

THIRD GENERATION

William Kinloch Anderson

A Hislop Anderson Jnr

FOURTH GENERATION

W J Kinloch Anderson

FIFTH GENERATION

Douglas Kinloch Anderson

Deirdre Kinloch Anderson

SIXTH GENERATION

John W Kinloch Anderson

Peter D Kinloch Anderson

Preface

This book commemorates the lifestyle and achievement of Kinloch Anderson, the tailoring and kiltmaking company that began as William Anderson & Sons in 1868. From its modest beginnings the Company progressed from a partnership between William Anderson and his two sons, to form a limited company which remains the Kinloch Anderson Company of today, managed by the fifth and sixth generations of the family.

Kinloch Anderson
SCOTLAND

Originally as civilian and military tailors Kinloch Anderson developed a particular expertise in tartans and kiltmaking and tailored officers' uniforms for all the famous Scottish Regiments. The Company has been instrumental in maintaining the profile and status of Highland Dress, both in Scotland and throughout the world. Today Kinloch Anderson have the finest selection of quality men's kilt outfits and accessories for Scotland's famous National Dress. Kinloch Anderson has also made a major contribution to many renowned companies, societies, institutions and individuals who value their identity expressed through exclusively designed tartans, clothing and accessories.

Particular pride is taken in the Royal Warrants of Appointment as Tailors and Kiltmakers to HM The Queen, HRH The Duke of Edinburgh and HRH The Prince of Wales. There has been a long and unbroken tradition of supplying the Royal Family, beginning with King Edward VII in 1903.

The Kinloch Anderson brand now has a unique place in the Scottish textile and fashion industry as a lifestyle heritage brand which it has developed in recent years mainly in the Far East with the brand image "The Best of British Styling and Fashion with a strong Scottish Emphasis", sometimes shortened to "British Style - Scottish Character".

The Company's history over nearly a century and a half is a history of Scottish fashion and Scottish culture.

It includes the development of many different divisions of the Company and many enterprising decisions to enter into new relationships and new markets. It is thanks to these developments that Kinloch Anderson has such a unique heritage and strong brand profile.

This publication tells the story of generations of individuals supporting the mission for excellence and sharing their knowledge and expertise with all who read it.

The philosophy of the company remains to be true to its ideals to provide quality merchandise together with a strong Scottish expertise in a global niche market.

The aim is to be a role model for Scotland, upholding the highest principles of integrity and service.

The Kinloch Anderson Company is proud of its long history and heritage and of continuing to this day to be an independent family run Company

Kinloch Anderson - Timeline

1860s

- William Anderson and his two sons ran a well known tailoring business in Edinburgh, the Capital City of Scotland. In 1868, with trade increasing, they decided to progress from their partnership by forming a Limited Company, thus founding the Kinloch Anderson Company of today.
- During the latter part of the 19th Century, Kinloch Anderson became renowned throughout the country and beyond, as Scotland's premier civilian tailors.

1900s

- In 1903 Kinloch Anderson first supplied the Royal Family – to King Edward VII.
- Prior to the advent of the First World War, military tailoring developed as an important part of the business, with officers' uniforms being tailored for all of the famous Scottish Regiments.

1930s

- In the 1930s, William Kinloch Anderson, the third generation Chairman, made an important decision to introduce ready-to-wear men's clothing – at that time a daring and innovative move for a prestigious tailor. Subsequently, as many other tailoring businesses declined, the Kinloch Anderson Company thrived as men's outfitters and specialists in Highland Dress
- Kinloch Anderson was granted their first Royal Warrant by King George V in 1934 and subsequently by King George VI in 1947.

1950s

- Kinloch Anderson appointed as Tailors and Kiltmakers to HM The Queen in 1955.
- The first visit of W J Kinloch Anderson, the fourth generation Chairman, to North America.
- In order to meet the increasing demand in the post war period, particularly in North America, a Wholesale Division was established to supply clothing and accessories in tartans and tweeds.

1960s

- The growth in manufacturing of quality men's and ladies' clothing, primarily for export to North America and European countries.
- Kinloch Anderson appointed as Tailors and Kiltmakers to HRH The Duke of Edinburgh in 1960.

1970s

- The first visit of Douglas Kinloch Anderson, the fifth generation Chairman, to Japan.
- With the high quality ladies' skirt business expanding in Europe and North America, Japan was the next market for export.
- In 1979 Kinloch Anderson exported £1 million worth of garments and was awarded the Queen's Award for Export Achievement.

1980s

- In 1980 Kinloch Anderson were appointed as Tailors and Kiltmakers to HRH The Prince of Wales.
- In 1983 The Company produced their first Corporate Uniforms and subsequently established their Corporate Identity Division. This Division has now expanded to provide Companies with a complete range of clothing and promotional gifts, in specially designed exclusive tartans.

- In 1983 Douglas Kinloch Anderson was awarded the OBE for Services to Export.

1990s

- As world markets became ever more sophisticated it was decided to develop the brand name and image of Kinloch Anderson by entering into Licence Agreements with compatible high quality partners – first in Japan, then in Taiwan and later in South Korea. These partnerships have blossomed and grown into a significant business in these countries.
- In 1999 Kinloch Anderson won the Award for Business Excellence as the best manufacturers and distributors in the Edinburgh and Lothians region of Scotland.

2000s

- John Kinloch Anderson, 6th generation, joined the company, and became Chief Executive in 2010.
- In 2010 Deirdre Kinloch Anderson was awarded the OBE for Services to the Textile Industry.
- Launch of the *Kinloch2* brand in South Korea.
- Launch of the *Kinloch by Kinloch Anderson* brand in South Korea.
- Kinloch Anderson Whisky Collection introduced into the Taiwanese marketplace.
- Launch of Kinloch Anderson's first online shop.
- Launch of new web site and online shop.
- In 2012 Peter Kinloch Anderson (John Kinloch Anderson's elder brother) joined the Company to be Director of Brand Development based in Shanghai to progress business in China and throughout Asia.

Every chapter is preceded by a different tartan from the *Kinloch Anderson Tartan Collection*.
The front side shows the tartan at full strength with the weave running from bottom left to top right.
The reverse side features the tartan – lightened in strength for artistic purposes – with the weave running
from bottom left.

Kinloch Anderson Tartan: page 13

Kinloch Anderson Castle Grey Tartan: page 29

Kinloch Anderson Hunting Tartan: page 41

Kinloch Anderson Rowanberry Tartan: page 53

Kinloch Anderson Black And White Tartan: page 67

Kinloch Anderson Romance Tartan: page 73

Kinloch Anderson Thistle Tartan: page 81

Kinloch Anderson Heather Tartan: page 97

Kinloch Anderson Dress Tartan: page 117

KINLOCH ANDERSON TARTAN

The Historic Journey of Highland Dress

To forbid the use of tartan by Act of Parliament seems incredible. Nevertheless it happened after Bonnie Prince Charlie's ill-fated attempt to seize the throne of Great Britain had ended in defeat at the Battle of Culloden in 1746. The Jacobite rising so alarmed the Government that among the measures adopted for pacifying the highlanders was a ban on wearing the kilt or dressing in tartan.

There were reasons for the decision. The primitive Highland Dress of those days allowed the hardy highlanders to climb hills and mountains, cross glens and bogs and fight on rough ground with unencumbered agility in all weathers : so it was considered to be a weapon of war. Furthermore, tartan material, being unique to the Highlands, was seen as a focus of loyalty to its wearers and a symbol of disloyalty to the Hanoverian government of Britain.

"From and after the first day of August one thousand seven hundred forty-seven," ran the Act, "no man or boy within that part of Great Britain called Scotland other than such as shall be employed as officers and soldiers in His Majesty's forces shall on any pretence whatsoever wear or put on the clothes commonly called Highland clothes (that is to say) the plaid Philebeg or little kilt, trowse, shoulder belts, or any part whatsoever of what peculiarly belongs to the Highland garb and that no tartan or party coloured plaid or stuff shall be used for great coats or for upper coats."

On conviction offenders were liable to be imprisoned for six months and, for a second offence to be transported for seven years "to any of His Majesty's plantations beyond the seas".

Those who were suspected, but not convicted, had to take this oath:

"I do swear … I … never use any tartan plaid or any part of the Highland garb and if I do so may I be cursed in my undertakings family and property – may I never see my wife and children, father, mother and relations – may I be killed in battle as a coward and lie without Christian burial in a strange land far from the graves of my forefathers and kindred – may all this come across me if I break my oath."

The repeal of the proscription came in 1782 and a Gaelic proclamation was displayed in the Highlands "LISTEN MEN This is bringing before all the sons of the Gael that the King and Parliament of Britain have ever abolished the Act against the Highland Dress that came down to the clans from the beginning of the world to the year 1746. This must bring great joy to every Highland heart. You are no longer bound down to the unmanly dress of the Lowlander. This is declaring to every man young and old simple and gentle that they may after this put on and wear the trews the little kilt the doublet and hose along with the belted plaid without fear of the law of the land or the spite of enemies."

Once again the Scots appeared in their beloved tartans.

Above: "An incident in the rebellion of 1745" by David Morier (1745 – 1785), showing men of the Jacobite army dressed in tartan kilts, jackets, waistcoats and trews in a great variety of unidentified tartans.

Not only had the Act failed to destroy Highland Dress, it had served to preserve it and pave a new pathway for it to develop in an unexpected direction. The Act specifically exempted "officers and soldiers in His Majesty's forces". Diverting the warlike energies of the highlanders into fighting for Britain rather than for the Jacobite cause had the added advantage of strengthening the army and pacifying the Highlands, and between 1757 and 1763 eleven Highland Regiments were raised, all of them "plaided and plumed in their tartan array." Feared by the enemy and admired by their allies , they were hugely successful in wars all over the British Empire and then in the struggle against Napoleon. When Sir Walter Scott visited Paris just after the battle of Waterloo he reported that "the singular dress of our Highlanders makes them particular objects of attention to the French."

The Highland Dress adopted by the military was colourful and unique, but neatly-tailored and correct by comparison with what had gone before. From the seventeenth-century onwards highland garb was little more than a belted plaid (the Gaelic word for "blanket"), a long rectangular piece of cloth roughly two yards wide and six yards long. It was belted and bunched round the waist with the upper section draped over the body – and over the head as well if necessary – allowing the arms complete freedom of movement. This Big Kilt (the "Feilidh-mor") could also be used as a blanket at night.

The kilt of today, as developed by the Highland Regiments, is a Little Kilt or "Feilidh-beg". It is the lower half of the plaid, stitched and pleated and with the front section replaced by two overlapping flat aprons. The upper section has become a detached plaid worn on the left shoulder and fastened with a brooch, and nowadays this is worn mainly by pipers.

Highland Dress would probably have remained solely a military uniform but for one man: Sir Walter Scott. The worldwide sales of his best-selling poems and novels introduced a particular vision of Scotland to the world, and as the result of his management of the royal visit to Edinburgh of George IV, the kilt became converted from a Highland Dress appropriate only to Highland regiments and gentlemen who lived north of the Highland line, to the Scottish National Dress, worn with pride by Scotsmen everywhere.

In 1800 books were expensive and the small reading public read the Bible, Homer and Virgil, Shakespeare's plays, history and sermons. The novel was in its infancy and for lighter reading there was only narrative poetry. In 1810 Scott's poem, *The Lady of the Lake*, took the reading public by storm and sold 20,000 copies in seven months. It was translated rapidly and swept Europe as well as America. Schubert set some of its songs to music (including "Ave Maria") and the Americans adopted "Hail to the Chief" as an unofficial anthem. Suddenly Scotland was interesting. The poem played into the growing fashion for rugged, romantic scenery; it introduced the world for the first time to the beautiful Scottish landscape around Loch Katrine, to romantic Scottish heroes and to battles amongst the heather. Needless to say most of the characters wore tartan!

The flames of tartan fever were fanned four years later by Scott's first historical novel, *Waverley*, and then by Rob Roy. The heroes of both were young

Englishmen who travelled north and found themselves involved on the Jacobite side of the Risings in 1715 and 1745.

As a letter to Scott from a French correspondent put it:

"Before your writings had reached the French shores, we Frenchmen were very little acquainted with Scotch topography, customs, laws and manners; now , there is a thirst for everything concerning the Scots, and a Parisian would be disgraced in society , were he to appear less familiar with Scottish affairs and places, than with French ones."

One of the most ardent admirers of Scott's poems and novels was Britain's Prince Regent who later, as George IV, paid the first modern Royal Visit to Scotland.

His Majesty came by sea and his ship arrived at Leith, the Port of Edinburgh at 2 p.m. on 14th August, 1822 – actually 4 days late. It was raining so the procession was cancelled until the following day.

It was when the ship was moored off shore that he first tried on his full Highland Dress outfit in the Royal Stewart tartan and appeared on deck wearing it. He found that it was too short for him because his girth was so large! That was why he decided to wear flesh coloured tights (which proved embarrassing for the ladies who speculated as to where on earth to look when they curtsied before him). When he set foot on shore the next day, however, he was attired as a British Admiral.

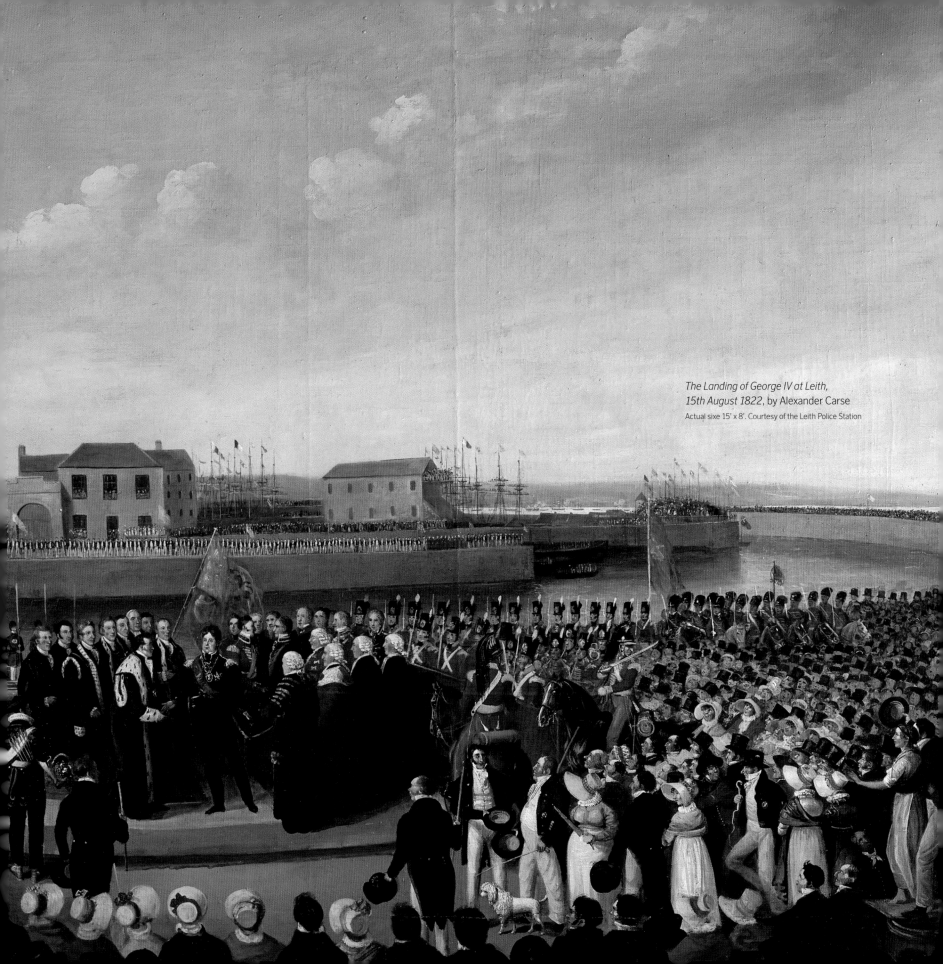

*The Landing of George IV at Leith,
15th August 1822*, by Alexander Carse

Actual sixe 15' x 8'. Courtesy of the Leith Police Station

Neither Sir Walter Scott, nor the vast majority of the 300,000 spectators, (a seventh of the whole population of Scotland) who were there to greet him were wearing tartan. Some of them followed the official suggestion that blue and white, as in the St Andrews Cross, would be appropriate.

Subsequently in the official processions that followed, however, there was tartan everywhere. Scott, who had been appointed by the Lord Provost to arrange and supervise the events for the visit, had written to a number of Highland gentlemen suggesting that they bring some of their dependents to join in the formal processions from Leith to Edinburgh and from Holyrood up the High Street to the Castle. So the great Officers of State, the regular soldiers, the High Constables and the judges found themselves amongst kilted members of the Celtic Society with gaggles of Highlanders attending on the Clan Chief of Glengarry and Sir Ewen McGregor, together with Breadalbane Highlanders and the Marischal Guard of Highland gentlemen. Not everyone approved of Sir Walter's ideas for "Celtified pageantry" but others such as Robert Mudie clearly did and wrote in an account of the visit:
"The judicious intermixture of the clans, with their tartan habiliments, and of the troops, formed a happy relief to the official splendour which marked other parts of the pageant".

It came as a complete surprise that the King adopted Highland Dress for these processions and the many Receptions that were held, including a levee at Holyrood Palace for more than 1,100 gentlemen. He had equipped himself well, however. The bill for his outfit from Hunter's of Edinburgh amounted to £1254.18s (close to £100,000 today). His purchases included two full Highland outfits, gold shoe rosettes "studded all over with variegated gems – a Powder horn with Variegated Scotch Gems and a Massive Gold Chain – a fine white Goatskin Highland Purse with massive Gold spring top and nine rich gold bullion Tassels and Cords – a Highland Dirk with knife and fork – a fine Basket Hilt Highland sword of Polished steel, Hilt and Mounting inlaid with gold – a pair of fine Highland Pistols inlaid all over and 109½ yards of Royal Stewart Tartan."

The important outcome was that he had given the seal of royal approval to the Scots way of dressing. Modern civilian Highland Dress became immediately fashionable and, like tartan, has scarcely been out of fashion since.

THE STORY BEHIND THE PAINTING
THE LANDING OF KING GEORGE IV AT LEITH, 15TH AUGUST 1822

The artist of this painting of the arrival of King George IV to Scotland on 15th August 1822 was Alexander Carse. He died in 1826 so the picture was probably painted in 1822 or the following year. Alexander Carse is better known for his pictures associated with Robert Burns, the most famous of which is entitled "The Holy Fair" and can be found in the Robert Burns Museum in Ayrshire.

Sir Walter Scott, the famous Scottish historical novelist, playright and poet of the 19th century, met George IV in London when he was Prince Regent. At that time George IV had never been to Scotland. He only had a romantic notion of Scotland through Sir Walter Scott's novels. Scott said that when he inherited the throne, the King should come to Scotland and thereby become the first sovereign to do so for over 160 years.

King George IV came by sea and the picture depicts him landing at Leith, the Port of Edinburgh. It should be noted that the painter has used artistic licence with regard to the figure of His Majesty, as he is shown to be elegantly lean, which was certainly not the case.

Sir Walter Scott wanted the King to be given the impression that the Scottish people were well-to-do, high-class citizens. So he was greeted by such people as the Lord Lieutenant, the Lord President of the Court of Sessions, the Lord Justice Clerk, the Sheriff's Depute of the County of Edinburgh, the Lord Chief Commissioner and the Procurator Fiscal – all of whom wore official regalia. Also on ceremonial duty for this occasion were the High Constables of Leith, the Royal Regiment of Infantry, the Royal Regiment of Scots Grey and the Royal Company of Archers (the King's Bodyguard in Scotland).

The Highland Clans were also to be present. They were instructed to wear their kilts but were told to keep their distance as they were still considered to be somewhat uncouth. The Clan Chief of Glengarry decided to disregard this request and rode up to the King's carriage, doffed his cap (the Glengarry) and welcomed King George IV to Scotland.

When he left Leith, His Majesty rode up to the High Street of Edinburgh and thereafter to Dalkeith House where a special gate called Kings Gate was built in honour of his visit, and also a "Flighting pond" for shooting ducks. He stayed there for two weeks until 29th August.

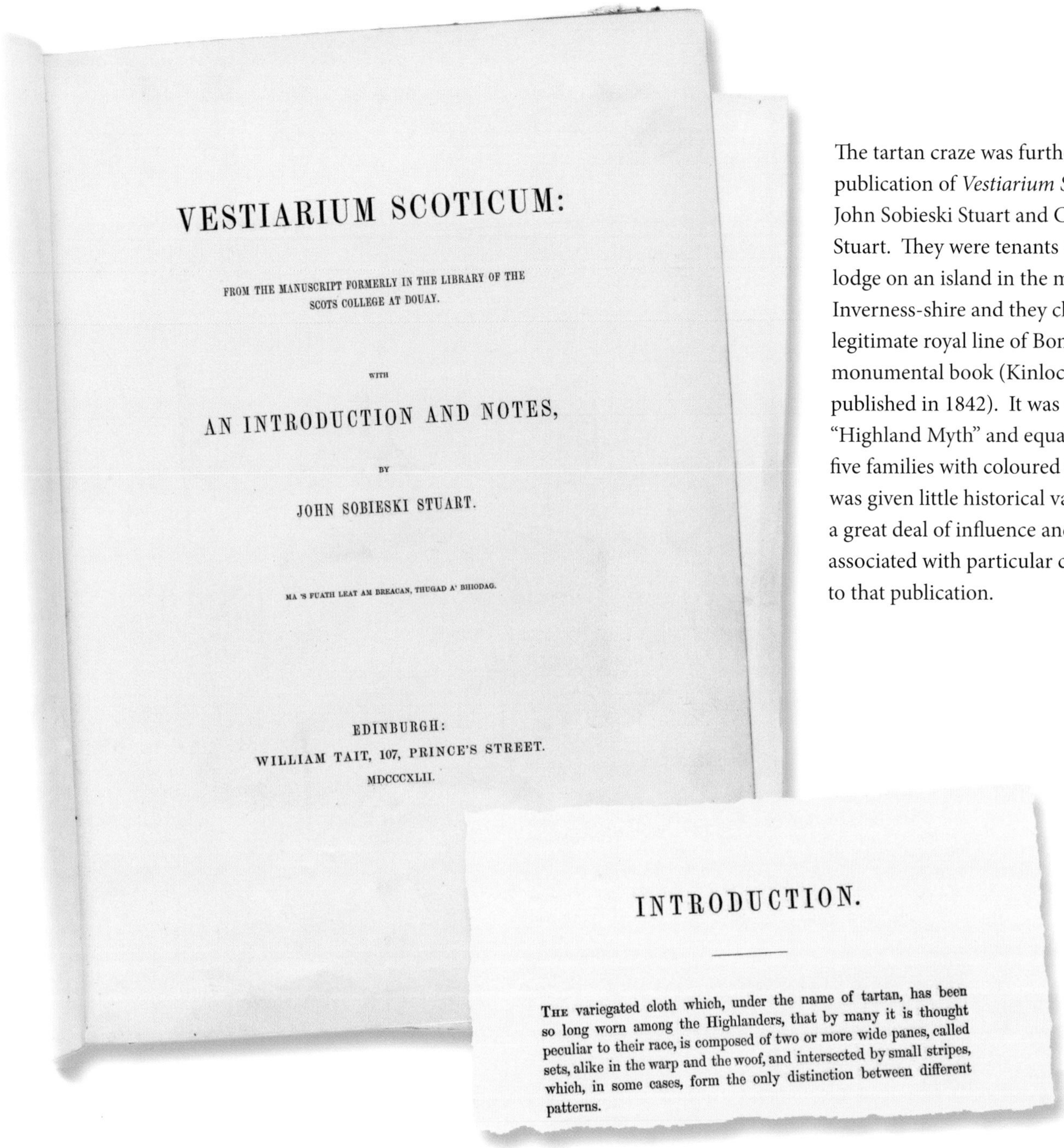

VESTIARIUM SCOTICUM:

FROM THE MANUSCRIPT FORMERLY IN THE LIBRARY OF THE
SCOTS COLLEGE AT DOUAY.

WITH

AN INTRODUCTION AND NOTES,

BY

JOHN SOBIESKI STUART.

MA 'S FUATH LEAT AM BREACAN, THUGAD A' BHIODAG.

EDINBURGH:
WILLIAM TAIT, 107, PRINCE'S STREET.
MDCCCXLII.

The tartan craze was furthered in 1829 with the publication of *Vestiarium Scoticum* by two brothers, John Sobieski Stuart and Charles Edward Sobieski Stuart. They were tenants of *Eilean Aigas*, an exotic lodge on an island in the middle of the River Beauly in Inverness-shire and they claimed to represent the legitimate royal line of Bonnie Prince Charlie. It was a monumental book (Kinloch Anderson have a copy published in 1842). It was at best accepted as "Highland Myth" and equally the account of seventy five families with coloured illustrations of their tartans, was given little historical validity. It did, however, have a great deal of influence and many of the tartans associated with particular clans and families date back to that publication.

INTRODUCTION.

THE variegated cloth which, under the name of tartan, has been so long worn among the Highlanders, that by many it is thought peculiar to their race, is composed of two or more wide panes, called sets, alike in the warp and the woof, and intersected by small stripes, which, in some cases, form the only distinction between different patterns.

Right:
The first paragraph of the "Introduction" is
an interesting early definition of tartan.

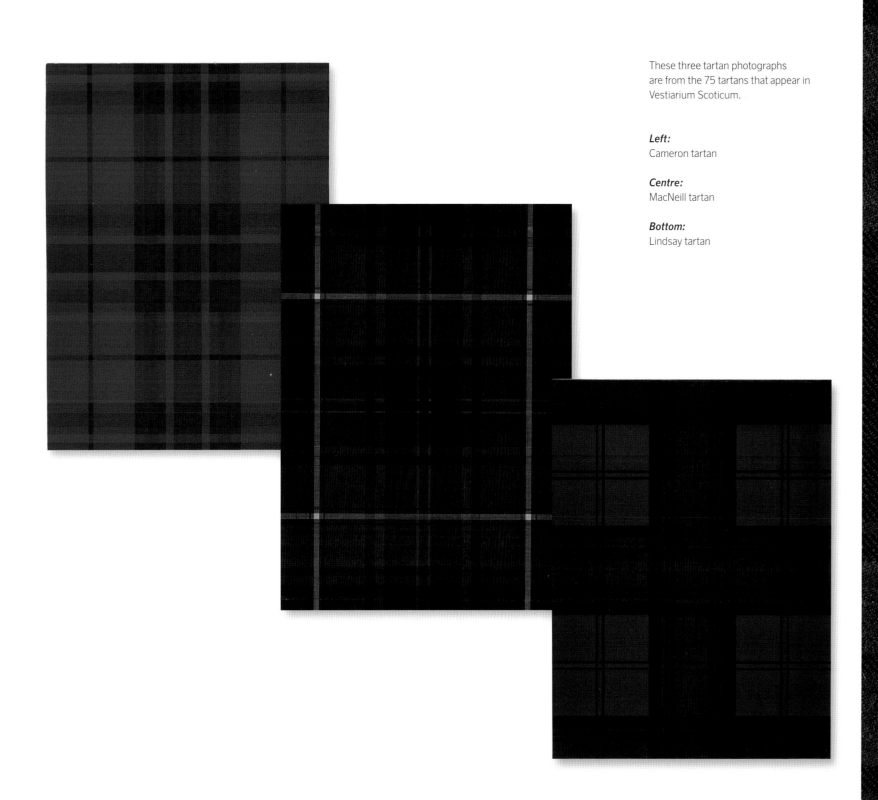

These three tartan photographs
are from the 75 tartans that appear in
Vestiarium Scoticum.

Left:
Cameron tartan

Centre:
MacNeill tartan

Bottom:
Lindsay tartan

THE SCOTTISH NATIONAL DRESS

Since earliest days, historic interest in Highland Dress has been essential to the Company's reputation and success. In the early 1900s a Handbook was published entitled "The Scottish National Dress for everyone interested in Highland Dress". It was written by the third generation owners, William Kinloch Anderson, his brother, William Hislop Anderson, and his son, W J Kinloch Anderson of the fourth generation. It ran to five editions and a copy is still to be found today in the National Library of Scotland.

The first Chapter entitled "The Origin and Development of Highland Dress" begins "The picturesque garb which has come to be regarded as the Scottish National Dress was a costume suited to the needs of a pastoral and warlike people in a mountainous country".

It continues to identify Highland Dress as "strikingly picturesque throughout the sartorial changes of each succeeding age" and states that it has remained "indeed fashionable and correct during a period when other masculine attire has become steadily less expressive and moreover is the reason why the kilt can be safely selected for virtually every occasion without the danger of incongruity or apprehension of being unsuitably dressed. The modern kilt of today is acknowledged to be the most striking and manly form of masculine attire".

Right:
The cover of this Handbook is after the original design by Robert Burns and features The Lion Rampant surrounded by Celtic design and the Cross of St Andrew.

THE MCLEAY BOOK

"The Highlanders of Scotland" was published in 1870. The artist Kenneth McLeay was a founder member of the Royal Scottish Academy in 1826.

Above and next page:
Illustrations from "The Highlanders of Scotland" 1870 edition. These are fine examples of the Victorian profile of Highland Dress.

KINLOCH ANDERSON CASTLE GREY TARTAN

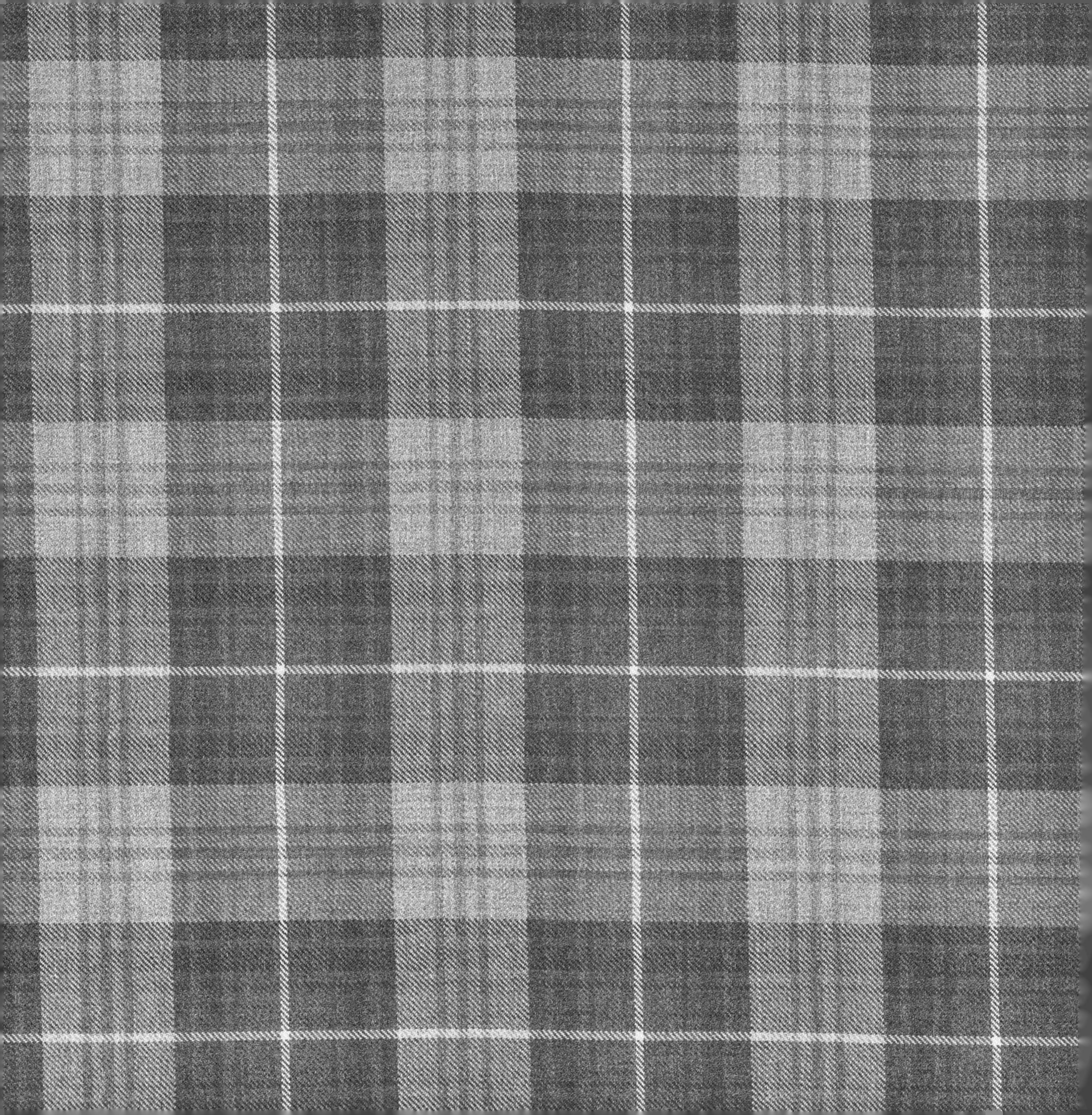

Uniforms for the Services

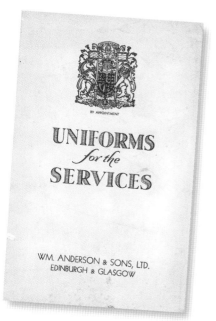

Before the Company changed its name to Kinloch Anderson, uniforms for the services were provided by William Anderson and Sons Limited from the time of the founding of the Company in 1868, throughout the period of the two world wars and into the second half of the 20th century.

Specialising in Scottish uniforms, the Company were regimental tailors to the regular officers of almost all the Scottish Regiments and the majority of territorial officers. William Anderson & Sons held every tartan used by the Scottish Regiments in stock.

a) b) c) d)

Above:
When the Company provided Uniforms for the Services it had a Royal Warrant of Appointment to HM King George V.

Left: Scottish Regiments of the Regular Army in the early part of the 20th century and their individual tartans.

a) Royal Scots 1942, Hunting Stewart tartan. Trews of the Government (Universal) tartan were worn from 1882 to 1901 when the tartan was changed to Hunting Stewart. The pipers wore Royal Stewart.

b) Royal Scots Fusiliers 1933. Government tartan.

c) The King's Own Scottish Borderers. Leslie tartan. From 1882 to 1898 trews of the Government tartan were worn. The Leslie tartan was adopted by the Regiment in 1898 to commemorate its first commander. From 1920 the pipers wore the Royal Stewart tartan.

d) The Cameronians 1927 (Scottish Rifles). Douglas tartan. Trews of the Government tartan were issued in 1882 but in 1892 the Douglas tartan was adopted for all ranks including pipers and drummers. The Earl of Angus, who raised the Cameronians, was a Douglas.

MILITARY TAILORING

Uniform Making is a branch of tailoring which demands Specialist knowledge. It is not knowledge easily acquired, and the necessary experience can only come after long practice.

Our Firm has been in existence since 1868, and our experience of Uniform Making covers practically this whole time. The period of the Great War enriched that experience, and to-day we can fully claim to be the premier Uniform Makers in Scotland. Naturally, we specialise in Scottish Uniforms. We are Regimental Tailors to the Regular Officers of practically all the Scottish Regiments, and we make for the large majority of Territorial Officers.

This Booklet is designed to show the scope of our Military Outfitting Service. It is not possible to show all details, but we are able to meet every Outfit need of the Military Officer. We invite your inquiries.

Our head office is in Edinburgh and we have a fully staffed branch in Glasgow. Our travelling representatives visit all parts of Scotland at regular intervals, and go to London, Aldershot, Dover, Catterick, or anywhere else a Scottish Regiment may be stationed.

Old Military Prints in our possession at George Street, Edinburgh

The Head Office was in Edinburgh but there was a fully staffed branch in Glasgow. Travelling representatives covered all parts of Scotland and also London, Aldershot, Dover and Catterick – anywhere where Scottish Regiments were stationed.

William Anderson and Sons claimed to be the premier uniform makers in Scotland and were recognised as Regimental tailors by the following Regiments: Royal Scots, Royal Scots Fusiliers,

Above

A page from the *Uniforms For The Services* booklet.

e) The Black Watch 1936 (Royal Highlanders). This Regiment was the oldest of the Highland regiments and wore the Government tartan, sometimes called the Black Watch. The pipers wore the Royal Stewart tartan.

f) The Highland Light Infantry 1929. MacKenzie tartan. In 1948 this regiment became a kilted unit continuing to wear the MacKenzie tartan.

g) The Seaforth Highlanders (Duke of Albany's) MacKenzie tartan.

e)

f)

g)

Kings Own Scottish Borderers, Cameronians (Scottish Rifles), Black Watch, Highland Light Infantry, Seaforth Highlanders, Gordon Highlanders, Cameron Highlanders, Argyll and Sutherland Highlanders.

When completed these paintings were submitted for critical approval by the Senior Officers of the Regiment concerned, thus ensuring absolute accuracy in all details.

They are still available to be seen in the Kinloch Anderson Heritage Room Museum in Leith, Edinburgh.

Alongside the provision of Full Dress Uniform for the Officers of the Scottish Regiments, the Company also supplied their uniform accessories which were called Regimental Ornaments. A complete set of "ornaments" consisted of sporran, dirk, sgian dubh,

Above:
A complete set of Regimental Ornaments.

h) The Gordon Highlanders. Gordon tartan. This regiment wore the Government tartan with a yellow overstripe.

i) The Queen's Own Cameron Highlanders 1927. Cameron of Erracht tartan. From 1943 the pipers wore the Royal Stewart tartan.

j) The Argyll and Sutherland Highlanders. The Government tartan in lighter shades.

Above:
Highland Dress Accessories Showcase showing:

- A Sgian Dubh supplied to the Queen's Own Cameron Highlanders.
- A Queen's Own Cameron Highlanders dirk to 1950 standard uniform regulations which includes a knife and fork.
- A Queen's Own Cameron Highlanders Officer's sporran.
- An Argyll and Sutherland Highlander's full dress hair sporran with five gold bullion tassels.
- A Gordon Highlander Officer's Sporran.
- A pair of shoes worn with Military Dress uniform.

shoulder brooch, full dress belts, and shoe buckles.

In the Kinloch Anderson Heritage Museum in Leith, Edinburgh there is a specific showcase showing some of the Company's historic collection of valuable Highland Dress accessories.

On 20th January 1959 the Royal Scots Fusiliers and the Highland Light Infantry were amalgamated to form the Royal Highland Fusiliers. This Regiment was known as Princess Margaret's Own Glasgow and Ayrshire Regiment and wore trews in the MacKenzie tartan (as did the Old Highland Light Infantry) and the Pipers wore the Dress Erskine tartan (adopted by the Royal Scots Fusiliers).

The Queen's Own Cameron Highlanders and the Seaforth Highlanders were also amalgamated to form the Queen's Own Highlanders (Seaforth and Camerons). All ranks wore either the Seaforth kilt or the Cameron tartan trews. The pipe and military bands wore the Cameron kilt and the Seaforth trews.

By 2004 there were just five remaining regiments – The Royal Scottish Borderers, The Royal Highland Fusiliers, The Black Watch, The Highlanders and The Argyll and Sutherland Highlanders. Then an interesting episode took place when in July 2004 the Government announced that all single battalion regiments were to form large regiments and this led to a considerable outcry in Scotland because it meant that the five remaining Scottish Regiments would be merged and therefore lose their individual identity and their regimental tartans.

Kinloch Anderson was approached by Colonel Robert Watson OBE who asked if the Company could find a way of designing a new composite tartan that would include elements of each of the existing regiments.

This tartan was therefore designed, woven and a sample kilt was made early in 2005. The design (right) is based on the sett of the Government tartan 1A worn by the Argyll and Suthertland Highlanders. It includes the red and yellow overcheck in the Hunting Stewart tartan worn by the Royal Scots, the red and white overcheck in the MacKenzie tartan worn by the Royal Highland Fusiliers and in the Leslie tartan

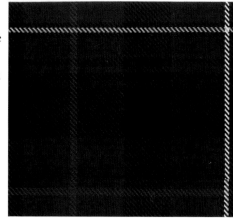

The composite tartan designed for the Royal Regiment of Scotland in 2006. It was never taken up.

SERVICE KIT

Left:
The Erskine Veterans tartan was launched by Squadron Leader Colin McGregor on 18th September 2006.

Above:
The Regular Army Service Kit.

worn by the King's Own Scottish Borderers, and the yellow overcheck is also found in the Gordon tartan worn by the Gordon Highlanders.

The Regimental Council strongly supported the idea but the Council of Scottish Colonels finally decided to adopt the Governement 1A tartan (similar to the Black Watch) and on 28th March 2006 the remaining regiments were merged to form The Royal Regiment of Scotland.

Fortunately the story did not end there. The composite tartan and the background story behind it became the basis for the Erskine Veterans tartan presented by Kinloch Anderson to the Erskine charity which cares for ex-service men and women. The Erskine Veterans tartan was launched by

Squadron Leader Colin McGregor at Lossiemouth on 18th September 2006.

In those previous times, the wealth of knowledge, experience and craftsmanship for making military uniforms and accessories for Parade kilts and Parade trews was also necessary for the Service Dress of Khaki Service Jacket, Khaki Plus 4s, Pantaloons, Grey Coat, Puttees, Sport hose tops, Sam Browne belt, Sporran and Glengarry.

Furthermore the reputation of the Company as Military Outfitters extended far beyond Scotland. Year by year, more officers of overseas Scottish Regiments were supplied by the Company who dealt regularly with units in Canada, South Africa, India and elsewhere in the Empire.

Right:
Sporrans supplied to overseas
and other regiments:

- 48th Highlanders of Canada
- Transvaal Scottish Volunteer
  Regiment (South Africa)
- Liverpool Scottish –
  a regiment formed
  from Scottish volunteers living
  in Liverpool circa 1900

Above:
Ties and squares in Regimental Colours.

Right:
The Service Waterproof Coat.

Far Right:
A feather Bonnet for Bands or Rank and
File Full Dress.

The following letter was received from the
Commanding Officer of a Canadian – Scottish
Regiment:

"I desire to assure you that the work has been most
satisfactory. It has not been necessary in any one
instance to have alterations made, which can only
be accepted as a tribute to the excellent
workmanship of your Firm, and to the careful
supervision given to all instructions."

Sporrans produced and sold to Regiments overseas
are still to be seen in the Kinloch Anderson
Heritage Room Museum.

Additional regimental clothing and equipment
included feather bonnets for Bands or Rank and
File Full Dress, and the service waterproof coat
fitted with saddle flap and leg straps, swords and
claymores, medals, uniform shirts, socks, gloves
and handkerchiefs, camp
and field equipment, boots
and shoes and airtight
uniform cases, and the list
would not be complete
without the mention of the
supply of ties and squares for
the RNER, RAF and all
Highland and Lowland
Regiments.

HIGHLAND REGIMENTS.

Published by

WILLIAM JONES & COMPY 236, REGENT ST LONDON.
Lacemen, Accoutrement Makers, Sword Cutlers and Manufacturers of Brooches, Dirks, Claymores, &c.,
CONTRACTORS.

Left:
"Highland Regiments" –
Illustration from the publication by William
Jones & Company, 236 Regent Street,
London, suppliers of military
accoutrements to the Company.

Right:
"Lord Lieutenant, Deputy Lieutenant, City Deputy".
Illustration from the publication by William Jones & Company, 236 Regent Street, London, suppliers of military accoutrements to the Company.

38   Uniforms for the Services

The Company's uniform tailoring expertise additionally extended to Civil and Diplomatic uniforms.

Uniforms were made for the Lieutenancy in every part of Scotland. The Lord Lieutenants and Deputy Lord Lieutenants deputised for the Sovereign when he or she was unable to attend official Royal functions in Scotland. The Company also supplied a large number of Royal Company of Archers outfits.

Many of the official uniforms were made for the Royal Household, civilian office bearers and voluntary brigades.

The Company supplied Court Dress and special coats for King's Counsels and Advocates, velvet Court Dress or Highland Court Dress for gentlemen present at Royal Courts and dress for Privy Councillors and for all classes of civil servants.

WM. ANDERSON & SONS, LTD., GEORGE STREET, EDINBURGH 2

WILLIAM ANDERSON

DEPUTY LIEUTENANT IN FULL LEVEE DRESS

DEPUTY-LIEUTENANTS AND VICE-LIEUTENANTS OF COUNTIES.

FULL DRESS.

WM. ANDERSON & SONS. EDINBURGH AND GLASGOW.

Above:
Royal Company of Archers modern border green uniform first introduced in 1829.

Top Left:
Mr William Kinloch Anderson, the third generation of the Company, was a member of the Queen's (Edinburgh) Rifle Volunteer Brigade and is wearing his Second Lieutenant's Uniform in 1895.

Left:
Deputy Lieutenant and Vice Lieutenant.

Far Left:
Deputy Lieutenant in Full Service Dress.

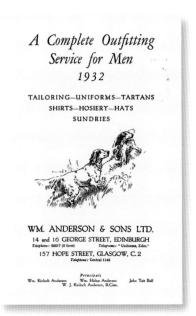

A Complete Outfitting
Service for Men
1932

TAILORING—UNIFORMS—TARTANS
SHIRTS—HOSIERY—HATS
SUNDRIES

WM. ANDERSON & SONS LTD.
14 and 16 GEORGE STREET, EDINBURGH
Telephone: 20517 (2 lines)   Telegrams: "Uniforms, Edin."
157 HOPE STREET, GLASGOW, C.2
Telephone: Central 1149

Principals
Wm. Kinloch Anderson   Wm. Hislop Anderson   John Tait Bell
W. J. Kinloch Anderson, B.Com.

It is hard to imagine how one small company could provide such a comprehensive range of uniforms, Court Dress and all the accompanying accessories. Yet William Anderson & Sons Ltd in 1932 had a complete Outfitting Service for men.

The range of goods and services provided included all of the following: tailored suits, overcoats, raincoats, hats and caps, underwear, shirts, collars and ties, sports kit, bathing costumes, pullovers and cardigans, pyjamas and dressing gowns, socks and stockings, gloves, handkerchiefs, tartan rugs, kilt outfits and

Above:
The Combination Sports Shirt

all Highland Dress accessories, travel equipment, trunks and suitcases, even trouser presses.

Our Aim is to provide service such as will give you entire satisfaction, and assure your continued patronage and recommendation. If in any particular transaction we have not accomplished this, you would do us a favour by pointing out where we have failed.

Every Order entrusted to us is under the personal charge of the head of the department concerned, who is in direct touch with the transaction until the customer is fully satisfied with his purchase.

Record of Particulars – A full record is kept of all particulars and measures. Repeat orders can always be executed promptly.

These were our Codes of Practice in the 19th century and they remain with us to this very day.

Right:
Pyjamas (and he's smoking!)

Far Right:
Ready-to-Wear or Made-to-Measure at William Anderson & Sons Ltd.

in harmony with your
SUITS

Ready - to - Wear
2 Collars with every Shirt
10/6   12/6   16/6

Made - to - Measure
in our own workrooms
2 Collars with every Shirt
18/6   25/-

TIES . . . 3/6 to 6/6

ASK FOR PATTERNS.

WM. ANDERSON & SONS LTD.
14/16 GEORGE STREET
EDINBURGH, 2
157 HOPE STREET
GLASGOW, C.2.

KINLOCH ANDERSON HUNTING TARTAN

The Heritage Story of Kinloch Anderson

by Douglas Kinloch Anderson

" William Anderson, while returning thanks for past favours, respectfully intimates that he has removed to those Central and Eligible Premises, No. 15 GEORGE STREET (opposite Commercial Bank), where he will continue, as he formerly did at North Bridge, personally to Superintend the Cutting Department. W. A. has assumed as Partners his Sons, WILLIAM and ANDREW, who have had considerable experience in every Branch of the Trade, and the Business will now be conducted under the Firm of WILLIAM ANDERSON & SONS. "

The Edinburgh Gazette, September 22nd 1868

Above:
Douglas Kinloch Anderson
Chairman of Kinloch Anderson
Joined the Company in 1962.

Left: The George Street Shop in 1890.

The story of Kinloch Anderson (formerly William Anderson & Sons) is something quite unique. It began in 1868.

The middle of the 19th century was a prosperous period in Edinburgh. Our founder, William Anderson and his two sons, William Joseph and Andrew Hislop, ran a tailoring business, supplying the needs of the worthy gentlemen of the City. It was doing well and they decided that the time was right to move from being a partnership to forming a Company.

William Anderson & Sons Ltd was established therefore in 1868 and initially business was conducted from premises in George Street where the George Hotel now stands. Soon the business moved across the street to a larger site at 14–16 George Street, which the Company occupied for over a century.

It is most unlikely at that time, that my great great grandfather imagined the business would still be in existence six generations later and into the 21st Century. Certainly he wouldn't recognise the business as it is today, with four divisions of the Company: Retail, Manufacturing and Wholesale, Corporate Identity and Brand Development in the Far East – and incidentally, 1868, the year of our foundation, was the year of the Meiji Restoration in Japan, then a far off country more or less closed to foreigners.

Right: HRH The Princess Royal inspects the DECS machine at the Restalrig Factory, Edinburgh. July 1988.

Bottom: Military Suppliers to the Scottish Regiments Overseas.

Military Kit for the East

			£3	15	0
Khaki Drill Jacket (buttons and rank badges extra)	. per set	0	3	6
Buttons	. per pair	0	2	0
Rank Badges	. per pair, from	0	1	6
Titles		1	4	6
Khaki Drill Shorts		1	1	0
Khaki Drill Slacks				
"Solaro" Sunproof All-wool Service Jacket, with regimental or	. from	7	0	0
leather buttons and 1 pair of rank badges				
Khaki Canton Riding Breeches, with knee strappings of same		3	7	6
material and buttons at knee		1	8	6
Khaki and White Helmets, regulation pattern		0	4	6
Spine Pads		2	10	0
White Mess Jacket	. from	1	2	0
White Mess Vest		1	12	6
Kummerbunds		2	15	0
White Dress Jacket, Stand Collar		1	15	0
White Overalls, with foot straps .		1	15	0
Green Mosquito Muslin Nets for ordinary camp bed, to fix		0	5	6
on rods		5	5	0
Mosquito Helmet Nets		0	3	6
Burberry .	. from			
Leather Waistbelts, all sizes				

(White Uniform, 7/6 per suit extra if fitted.)

Shirts, Collars, Underwear, Hosiery, etc.—see pages 24 to 40.

Foreign Outfitting Booklet sent on request.

WM. ANDERSON & SONS, LTD.
EDINBURGH and GLASGOW

57

Our Digital Electronic Chalking System (DECS for short) would never have entered his mind as being an important piece of equipment which enabled us to become world leaders in the perfection of pleating tartan skirts. Nor would he have imagined the Edinburgh Zoo Panda tartan being designed specially to commemorate the arrival from China of two giant pandas for the Edinburgh Zoo.

For many, the image of Kinloch Anderson is as being classic and traditional. I suggest that change is the key to why the Kinloch

Anderson Company continues to exist, and to thrive, six generations later. Inevitably the Company has moved with the times in a general sense but more importantly critical decisions have been made at critical times in the emphasis of the business and these have been vital in the evolution of the Company. Obviously not all the moves have been the right ones, mistakes have been made along the way and opportunities have been missed. It is easy to look back and wonder why a particular course of action was or was not taken at some crucial stage - and I suppose all of us can identify with that to some extent in our own lives.

Nonetheless as far as Kinloch Anderson is concerned, the fact is that enough of the right critical decisions have been taken along the way, and it is worth looking at some of these to see how the Company has evolved and changed direction over its 145 year history.

In its early years, the Company prospered as bespoke tailors of fine clothes for the gentlemen of Edinburgh and many well-to-do people all over Scotland. Military tailoring became a speciality with Officers' uniforms being tailored for all the Scottish Regiments, as well as for the regiments in India and other various parts of the Empire, such as The Transvaal Scottish and The Toronto Highlanders.

THE BLAZER AND FLANNEL TROUSERS
No better coat garment can be had for golfing than a good easy-fitting Blazer. For warm weather a Blazer and Flannel Trousers are ideal.

Quotations given for Clubs or Societies. Special Badges and buttons can be supplied.

HOSIERY AND SHIRT DEPARTMENT

*I*N this department you will find the latest designs and styles in the best qualities—with an expert staff ready to give you courteous assistance. The stock is large and varied and includes—

Shirts—Made to Measure or Ready to Wear

All measurements are recorded, so that repeat garments can be made at any time

Sports Caps and Hats 8/6 to 17/6

THE LOUNGE SUIT

THE PLUS-FOUR SUIT

Above: 1930s gentleman's tailoring:-
The blazer and flannel trousers
The Lounge Suit
The Plus-Four Suit

Left: A staff group in the 19th century

a)

The Company was renowned as the largest military tailors in Scotland, with at one time over 200 fully timeserved and qualified tailors sitting cross legged on their benches in their workshop.

In our Heritage Museum in Leith, you can see the original paintings of the uniforms. Also in large leather bound pattern books there are cloth cuttings taken for every piece of tartan cloth woven.

The significance of the move from civilian bespoke tailoring to military tailoring is that this is the origin of the Company's special knowledge about kiltmaking, Highland Dress and Tartans – elements which are still of great importance to the Company today.

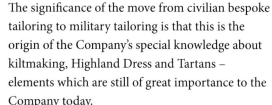

Above:
The Highland Light Infantry Regimental Uniform 1929.

a) and b): These are from a collection of five Haswell Miller Prints which were commissioned by the Company in 1952. They are thought to have been produced to help check that every detail of the uniform was correct.

Right: Tartan pattern books.

Far Right
c): Velvet Coatee with plaid, jabot and ruffles
d): The Doublet

Extreme Right: The Scottish National Dress, *A Handbook for Everyone interested in Highland Dress* by Wm Anderson & Sons in 1920.

A bold move was made by my grandfather during the late 1920s. For the first time, he introduced ready-to-wear suits to meet the growing demand for this new and innovative product. This move incurred the wrath and disdain of the Master Tailors in George Street (there were 17 of them at the time) who considered that the owner of our prestigious tailoring business had taken leave of his senses to go 'down market' in such a way by introducing ready-to-wear clothing.

He was right, however, and the Company enjoyed a prosperous period as the premier men's outfitters in Edinburgh, whilst the demand for tailor-made clothes gradually declined, and one by one the other George Street tailors faded away.

The Black Watch Regimental Uniform 1936.

WM. ANDERSON & SONS, LTD.   EDINBURGH AND GLASGOW

c) THIS illustration shows a Velvet Coatee, the belted Plaid, and the Jabot and Ruffles. This Coatee has the old-world style of front, which may also be used on the Doublet.

d) THIS illustration shows the most usual style of Doublet. The Doublet is an alternative style to the Coatee, and is specially suitable for the man of big build.

This brings me to the second key factor to the long life of the Company – we established ourselves as specialists in a 'niche' market. The Company became the recognised authority on Tartans and Highland Dress, as illustrated by a company publication – not a sales catalogue but a serious booklet entitled *The Scottish National Dress* which ran to many editions and which can be found in the National Library of Scotland.

Another milestone in the Company's history took place in the immediate post-Second World War era. Strong connections with many of the Canadian regiments meant that senior members of the Company, including my father, the fourth generation, travelled frequently to Canada (on lengthy six weeks trips by ship) to service the Officers both for their uniform and civilian needs.

During these visits in the late 1940s and 1950s, enquiries were being received from new retail shops opening up in Canada in the post war era, seeking supplies of tartans, tweeds and clothing.

The SCOTTISH NATIONAL DRESS

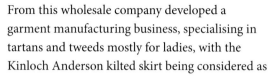

From this wholesale company developed a garment manufacturing business, specialising in tartans and tweeds mostly for ladies, with the Kinloch Anderson kilted skirt being considered as the market leader. Markets were soon developed in the USA as well as Canada, and Bermuda and throughout Europe with Italy, France, Germany, Austria and Switzerland as key countries.

In the boom times of the 1970s and 1980s, over 100,000 garments a year were leaving Edinburgh for the world's best stores and shops

The Scottish textile industry as we know it today did not exist, so our Company set up a wholesale subsidiary to meet this new and expanding business potential. This was actually the first time that the name "Kinloch Anderson" was used. One or two other small companies were acquired. Connachie & Co specialised in woollen goods and Nicoll Bros. made sporrans and leathergoods. So Kinloch Anderson set off in a new direction. This was at a time when the future of 'one off' independent menswear retailers was under increasing threat from the development of the multiples.

from New York to San Francisco, from Montreal to Paris, from Munich to Oslo and from Rome to Vienna, and a tentative toe was dipped into the markets of the Far East in Japan. Other Scottish clothing and accessories were also exported at that time mostly for Scots living in North America or to the American tourist market in Bermuda and for many years Kinloch Anderson owned and ran its own shop, Scotland House, in Alexandria, Virginia.

Left:
Kinloch Anderson Menswear Shop

Bottom Left:
Kinloch Anderson childrenswear Shop

Bottom:
Kinloch Anderson Leathergoods

World recession, and changes away from classic fashion slowed the growth, but an important change of direction for the Company had again taken place - this time it was the involvement with Japan and the Far East. In addition to exporting clothing and other merchandise made by Kinloch Anderson in Scotland it was realised that there was potential to develop licensee partnerships with top quality manufacturers to produce and market merchandise under the Kinloch Anderson brand name in their respective countries.

It started in Japan in the 1980s and in the 1990s these developments expanded into Taiwan and South Korea with a major project of expansion in China which commenced in 2012. Licensee partnerships were developed for menswear, ladieswear, childrenswear, leather goods, shoes, household textiles and accessories such as umbrellas, gift items and watches. There are now more than 300 Kinloch Anderson shops in Asia developed in co-operation with the Company's Design Team here in Scotland, and all reflecting the brand image of the best of British style and fashion with a Scottish emphasis – British Style, Scottish character.

This brings me to another key to survival over the years – having a complementary balance of activities which are different but related, such that if one is struggling, the others will support it, and vice versa. In recent years we have adopted this as a positive strategy for the Company.

The development of our Corporate Identity Division has increased in importance – especially in the last few years. This stemmed from the increasing demand for companies and other organisations to express their identity through the

creation of their own exclusive tartan. British Caledonian (Caledonian Airways) were probably our first significant Corporate customer. There are a multitude of uses for a corporate tartan – staff uniforms, corporate gifts, PR, and merchandise for resale. The combination of Kinloch Anderson's knowledge, and manufacturing capacity makes us particularly well equipped to develop this business,

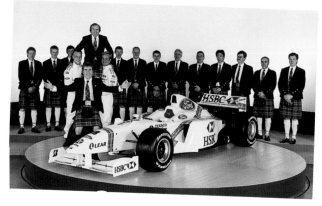

and we have undertaken projects for many well known companies and organisations – Chivas Regal, Glenlivet, The Royal College of Surgeons of Edinburgh, The Old Course Hotel St Andrews, Scottish Brewers, Barbour, Irn Bru, The Commonwealth Games, The Scottish Register of Tartans, the Institute of Directors, Napier University, the City of Edinburgh and many others.

Tartan is Scotland's own special identity and it is an identity that has spread throughout the world. People both expect to see it and want to feel it when they come to Scotland, Companies recognise its value and work with us to help us respond to their needs. Our tartan heritage and the importance of tartan to the Kinloch Anderson

Above:
British Caledonian Airways – Uniforms from 1985.

Right:
The Basel Tattoo (Official) tartan

Far Right:
Paul Stewart, Sir Jackie Stewart and the 1998 Stewart Grand Prix Team wearing Racing Stewart tartan outfits supplied by Kinloch Anderson.

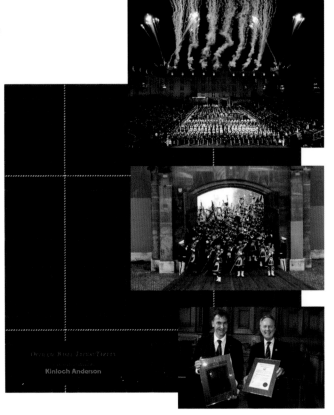

image and profile cannot be underestimated. A short history of tartan, the foundation of *The Scottish Register Of Tartans* and the tartans associated with the Royal Family are covered separately in this book.

The original activity of Kiltmaking and Highland Dress remains central to the Company's image and activities – and we are proud to have been granted Royal Appointments as Tailors and

Kiltmakers to HM The Queen, HRH The Duke of Edinburgh and HRH The Prince of Wales.

Highland Dress has experienced a huge resurgence of interest in the past twenty years or so, particularly with young people. We have grasped this opportunity in a number of ways – for instance, we have expanded our Kiltmaking capacity and also we have recognised the desire of younger people to wear a Kilt for leisure and

sporting occasions with the "Breacan".

The Breacan was developed specifically to meet the Scots' desire to dress in tune with today's more casual way of dressing. It is not a substitute for the traditional kilt but nevertheless maintains Kinloch Anderson's high quality production standards and represents one of the other factors of progress – the combination of traditional skills with modern values. So the products may have evolved and the customers may have changed, but the quality of our merchandise and the quality of our service have not been compromised over the years.

Opportunities have arisen when we could have made large sales if we had modified quality and reduced our prices (piled it high and sold it cheap). That has not been our policy. Integrity of business practice and loyalty from staff, suppliers and customers have all contributed to our continued progress over 145 years.

Above:
The Breacan - a kilted garment for leisure and sporting occasions.

Top Left:
Kiltmaking production at Leith.

Middle Left:
A Kinloch Anderson family group at The Gathering in Holyrood Park, Edinburgh, July 2009.

Left:
A formal Kinloch Anderson Highland Dress outfit.

Above:
Deirdre Kinloch Anderson
1990 Sales and Promotion Executive
1992 General Manager
1995 Director

Above:
John Kinloch Anderson
2000 Brand Development Manager
2003 Sales and Marketing Director
2007 Deputy Chairman
2010 Chief Executive

A new era began in 1990 when my wife, Deirdre, a fellow graduate from St Andrews University joined the Company. She had always taken a great interest and given her support in many ways, frequently accompanying me on business visits to Europe, North America and the Far East, and also by hosting the return visits to Scotland from overseas agents and contacts. She joined the Company, initially on a part time basis and incrementally took full time responsibilities in Sales and Marketing before becoming a Director and subsequently the Senior Director of the Company.

The next important milestone was the introduction of the sixth generation when our younger son, John, joined the Company in 2000 at the age of 29. As a graduate from Loughborough University he had already acquired several years of business experience in London. He brought with him a new outlook with new skills and in particular, expertise in IT and digital communications. He was appointed Chief Executive in 2010.

It had become increasingly clear that the significant developments in Asia required more than periodic visits from Scotland and in 2012 our elder son, Peter, joined the Company after a career in Hotel and Cruise Line Management, latterly in Miami, USA. He joined to fulfil the role of Kinloch Anderson's Director of Brand Development for Asia, based in Shanghai. So we are presently at another crucial stage in the development of the Company. We have a longevity and expertise in the field of Scottish clothing and textiles that is without equal and we remain family owned and managed. The development of our lifestyle brand is increasingly important to us both in terms of its financial contribution and for the global recognition it gives to the Company name.

These are exciting times for Kinloch Anderson and together with the support of our loyal and committed staff we now look forward to developing our considerable potential for many generations to come.

Below:
Peter Kinloch Anderson
2012 Director of Brand Development

KINLOCH ANDERSON ROWANBERRY TARTAN

Highland Dress in Modern Times

Highland Dress in the 21st century has changed little from the Scottish garments of the previous two centuries, retaining the same essential features. Yet each generation has introduced modifications and new fashions have inevitably exerted some influence. Interestingly, Highland Dress today has rediscovered some of the practical and artistic advantages of the early styles which became more elaborate and highly decorated in the 19th century.

Kinloch Anderson have been at the forefront of responding to the changing tastes and conditions as they have occurred in each of the preceding generations. If asked to do so by their customers, it is the Company policy to provide expert advice and carefully considered opinions based on past traditions and current trends. It is not the Company's position, however, to assert views against others who may think differently nor to openly criticise other "interpretations". Most of these will probably disappear as rapidly as they came.

Information that is provided regarding which tartan to wear is based on accurate historic sources associated with the great Scottish families and linked to the Scottish Clan system and its traditions. Kinloch Anderson have extensive records and are always ready to explain and advise. One tartan name may have a number of options and colourways such as modern, ancient, muted, weathered (or reproduction), hunting, or dress. Kinloch Anderson can show and explain them all.

In the absence of a claim to the name of a particular tartan, there is a range of alternative "universal" or other tartans which are available or even a plain or shadow fabric or a tweed if preferred.

Highland Dress belongs to culture and not to science. It remains a question of personal free choice both as to whether it may be worn and in what manner. For Kinloch Anderson the most important issue of all is that it is treated with pride and respect because for us it is "the finest National Dress in the world".

Above: Kinloch Anderson Highland Dress in the early 20th century.

Left: Kinloch Anderson Highland Dress in 21st century.

Highland Dress outfit worn with black tie for evening dress.

The Kilt

In the earliest times the key features of Highland Dress were the kilt and the plaid. For most Scotsmen today, however, the 'jewel in the crown' is the kilt itself. The kilt has never become archaic because it encompasses such a variety of tartan designs and colours. This gives it an individuality not readily found in other types of dress where high fashion shapes and colours change in popularity in over a matter of years.

Highland Dress is by nature versatile and the diversity of the kilt is expressed through the fabric. Whilst pipe band members and those who essentially want to wear the kilt outdoors in cold climates may prefer to choose a heavy weight wool worsted tartan, the best kilt fabric for most people today will be a firm wool worsted fabric rather than a Saxony or softer wool fabric. The firmness of the fabric means that when the pleats have been strongly pressed they will remain in place during long hours of use. The other criteria for this is the depth of the pleats themselves – the deeper the pleats the better they stay in place.

There are several ways in which a kilt can be pleated – pleated to sett, line pleated or box pleated. These will be explained later in the Chapter on kiltmaking.

The Breacan

The 'Breacan' is a kilted garment which has been designed by Kinloch Anderson specifically to meet the Scot's desire for a garment in tune with today's more casual style of dressing. It is not intended as a substitute for the traditional kilt, which continues to grow in popularity, but provides an alternative particularly suitable for many leisure and sporting occasions.

Highland Dress Jackets and the Kinloch Anderson Jacket for Trousers

Highland Dress jacket styles have been adapted over the years in line with modern conditions of use. The Doublet, the jacket (or Coatee) and indeed the headwear have varied according to the fashion of each succeeding period. In the 17th century the elaborate slashed

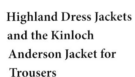

doublet of the Restoration was worn. The mid-18th century brought about a succession of velvet and tartan doublets and coatees, some of which are only slightly modified today. Whilst we can trace mediaeval, Jacobean, Georgian and Victorian influences on modern styles it was the styles of the mid-18th century which formed the natural basis of the modern styles of today. Interestingly Highland Dress jackets have been differentiated for formalwear, semi-formalwear and daywear and the same applies to the sporran, the belt and buckle, the sgian dubh and even the kilt pin.

Daywear Jacket

All kilt jackets are shorter than the normal man's jacket because the kilt is worn 2" above the waist – this is called the kilt rise – and eliminates any "gap" showing between the kilt and the jacket. The daywear kilt jacket is quite simple, traditionally made from green or blue Lovat tweed but also from Harris Tweed, brown Lovat tweed or other tweeds.

Kinloch Anderson have specifically responded to the demand for a Charcoal tweed jacket which is extremely smart and particularly suitable for daytime weddings. The day jacket has staghorn buttons and can be worn open or fastened at the top button.

ANDERSON'S

Above:
Daywear in the early 20th century.

Above Left:
The Kinloch Anderson Breacan worn with a green Jacobite shirt.

Far Left:
Daywear in the 21st century.

Left:
The Kinloch Anderson Charcoal tweed jacket and waistcoat.

Above:
The Kinloch Anderson Coatee and Vest in the early 20th century.

Right:
The Kinloch Anderson Argyll Jacket.

Bottom Right:
The Kinloch Anderson Coatee and Vest in the 21st century.

Below:
Kinloch Anderson's Celtic button formation on the tails of the Coatee and Vest.

The Argyll Jacket

Usually made in Black Barathea a fine 100% wool cloth, this semi-formal jacket is popular because it is so versatile and suitable to be worn in daytime with a plain or Club tie or with a black bow tie for eveningwear and formal occasions. The Celtic buttons on the jacket and the gauntlet cuffs are ornamental and also feature on the specially shaped pocket flaps.

The Coatee and Vest

Without doubt this short neat formal jacket is shown as representing the National Dress of Scotland more than any other jacket. It is usually made in Black Barathea with silk facings on the lapels but can also be made in other colours and fabrics and is always accompanied by a "vest" which either matches the jacket or can be in tartan or another colour. Quite a recent name for this jacket is a Prince Charlie, although this is similar but not identical to it. The Coatee and Vest is without epaulettes (a plaited band on the shoulder) and the 4 Celtic buttons on each side of the tails at the back are arranged in the traditional pattern formation shown below. Although it has 3 Celtic buttons, these are never fastened and there are also 3 Celtic buttons on the jacket cuffs. The Vest (Waistcoat) is fastened with 3 Celtic buttons.

Montrose Doublet

A Barathea fabric or rich velvet is usually used for this jacket. This is a double breasted short cut evening jacket with high collar. It has 10 symmetrically positioned Celtic buttons on the front, 3 Celtic buttons on each cuff and epaulettes with Celtic buttons on each shoulder. This jacket is worn with a belt and normally with lace jabot and cuffs.

Kenmore Doublet

The Kenmore Doublet was first designed by Kinloch Anderson (William Anderson & Son Ltd at that time) in the early 1900s and was a simplified

form of the then "old fashioned Doublet". This is a single breasted evening jacket with high collar worn with a belt. There are flaps at the back and the front with 3 Celtic buttons and 2 Celtic buttons at the centre back. The front fastens with 5 Celtic buttons, there are 3 Celtic buttons on each cuff and a Celtic button on the epaulettes. This jacket is normally worn with lace jabot and cuffs and is most frequently made in Black Barathea fabric.

Sheriffmuir Doublet

This is a high collared evening jacket worn with jabot and cuffs and most frequently made in a rich velvet fabric. The top button can be fastened or left open. There are Celtic buttons down the cut-away front also on the front and back flaps, on the cuffs and on the epaulettes. This Doublet is usually worn with a matching or tartan 7-button waistcoat.

Bottom Left:
The Montrose Doublet.

Left:
The Kenmore Doublet.

Bottom:
The Sheriffmuir Doublet

Above:
The Kinloch Jacket.

Right:
Tartan Evening Waistcoat cut on the bias.

Top Right:
The Regulation Doublet.

Regulation Doublet

A rich velvet fabric is normally selected for this low break point, open jacket with low fastening waistcoat. The Celtic buttons are positioned diagonally on the front and also feature on the flaps on the front and back, the gauntlet cuffs, the epaulettes and the waistcoat.

The Kinloch Jacket

The Kinloch jacket is exclusive to Kinloch Anderson and has been specifically designed to wear with tartan trousers. Based on a blazer style with 2 lower pockets and a breast pocket and a double vent at the back, the jacket is longer than other kilt jackets but slightly shorter than a standard blazer. In tune with kilt jackets it features 3 Celtic buttons on the cuffs and fastens with 2 Celtic buttons at the front.

Highland Dress Waistcoats

These can be made either in the same fabric as the jacket or in tartan. Tartan waistcoats are often preferred to be cut on the bias. The Day Waistcoat has a high breakpoint and 5 Celtic buttons and the Evening Waistcoat has lapels, a low breakpoint and 3 Celtic buttons.

The Plaid

The Plaid evolved from the top half of the "Great" kilt when this was separated into the "Little" kilt and the plaid. It therefore has considerable traditional implications and today its swinging folds enhance the outfit with an additional sense of pride to the wearer.

The Piper's Plaid continues to manifest itself extensively in pipe bands whereas individuals will select a Fly Plaid for weddings and other ceremonial occasions.

The Fly Plaid is traditionally purled fringed but can also be plain fringed. It is usually made from 1.5 metres square of tartan, gathered at one corner and attached at the gathered centre with a brooch just below the top of the left shoulder.

Tartan Trousers

When the *Scottish National Dress* booklet was first published by William Anderson and Sons in the early 1900s there was no reference to tartan

trousers. However, as Highland Dress experts today Kinloch Anderson also respond to an ever increasing number of requests for tartan trousers, made to order in the tartan of the customer's choice and in his preferred style of trouser.

Whenever "tartan" and "trousers" are written together it invariably becomes "tartan trews". However trews strictly belong to the military. The trouser leg is straight cut without a second outside seam, and a narrow plain coloured band frequently runs straight down the outside of the leg from top to bottom (particularly with the military). It is an elegant trouser for the very slim; for the not so slim it is indeed a tailoring challenge.

What most people wear today are tartan trousers and frequently chosen by those who feel hesitant to wear the kilt, preferring their legs to be covered!

Tartan trousers can be worn formally at a Highland Ball or a traditional Scottish event with the Kinloch jacket or even an Argyll jacket. If the customer wants to wear them with the Coatee and Vest then he is advised to choose fishtail back trousers which are high waisted and help to eliminate any "gap" between the jacket and the trousers. The Celtic buttons on all these jackets enhance the Scottish nature of the tartan trouser outfit. However, tartan trousers can equally well be worn informally to a sporting event or gathering both indoors and outdoors once again emphasising their versatility in the modern world of today.

Left:
Fly plaid worn with a formal Eveningwear outfit.

Below:
Kinloch Anderson tartan trousers worn with a green velvet Smoking Jacket.

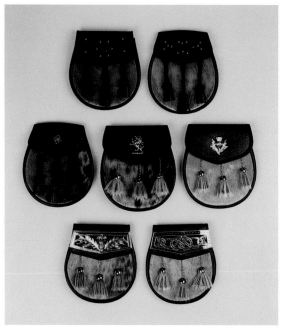

The Inverness Cape

Whilst it is perfectly acceptable to wear an ordinary overcoat over Highland Dress, the traditionally correct garment is the Inverness Cape, a full loose cape with a removable hood, usually made in Black Barathea. It began as a top coat with sleeves covered by a long cape. In the 1880s the sleeves were removed and the armholes cut away beneath the cape to enable the wearer to access his sporran without opening up the cape – and this became the Inverness Cape of today. The Inverness Cape has now been almost universally adopted by pipe bands for wet weather.

HIGHLAND DRESS ACCESSORIES

The Sporran

Originally, the Sporran was quite a large, somewhat, clumsy pouch made from the skin of an animal such as an otter or a goat, and used for storing oats or other food. Later other types of sporran came to include animal masks made from badger, otter, fox and pine martin, with the head

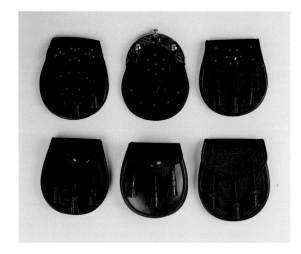

forming the flap that folds over the front and closes the sporran; these are rarely seen today due to contemporary views on animal rights. For people of importance a sporran would be mounted with brass or silver in previous times, but today the sporran has become a finely ornamented accessory used to hold such items as money, keys and handkerchiefs. Every sporran has two leather and chain straps and buckles attached to rings on the back of the sporran. The straps are then put through the sporran loops at the back of the kilt. The hang of the sporran can be adjusted to be worn high and not mid-way down the front of the kilt. As with Highland Dress jackets, sporrans are now classified differently according to the occasion and the time of day. So there are Day Sporrans, Semi-Dress Sporrans and Dress Sporrans.

Day Sporrans are normally entirely made from black or brown leather with leather tassels. The front of the sporran can be plain or studded (tooled) and in most cases the sporran fastens with a flap.

Above:
Inverness Cape in Black Barathea

Centre:
Day Sporrans

Top Right:
Semi Dress Sporrans

Below:
Animal head musquash sporran shown here from 1920s This is no longer acceptable as Highland Dress accessory.

Semi-Dress sporrans were traditionally made from leather and sealskin as seals are to be found in abundance around the northern shores of Scotland. In 2010 legislation was introduced to protect seals, banning the use of sealskin for all items including sporrans. It was designed to bring Scotland into line with other EU members where the law already applied to animals like badgers, deer, wild cats, hedgehogs, bats, links, moles, seals, whales, dolphins and porpoises. The ban on the use of sealskin meant that other skins which previously had limited use are now becoming more prevalent, for example bovine and pony. Semi-Dress Sporran tassels can be made in leather or matching skin cones with chains. The sporran flap is frequently more ornate with designs such as the Lion Rampant, Celtic and Scottish Thistle.

Dress or evening Sporrans team their use of leather with more exotic skins such as mink, chinchilla, skunk, possum, nutria, fox, Tibetan goat or sometimes synthetic fur. The tassel cones match the fine metal or sterling silver cantle which is usually quite ornate. The Dress Sporran is renowned for its distinguished grand appearance, probably due to Victorian times when these sporrans became ostentatious and much more elaborate than in previous centuries.

Below:
Dress Sporrans

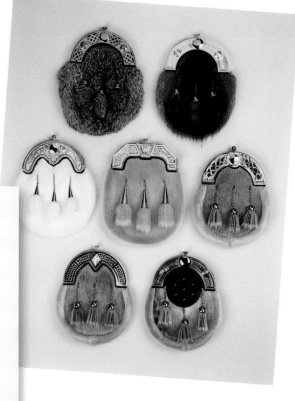

Left:
A selection of Sporrans on sale at interesting prices in the early part of 20th century.

DAY SPORRANS

THE photographs on this and the opposite page illustrate a number of the styles of Sporrans which we keep regularly in stock. Special designs of any kind can be produced, and sketches and estimates will be sent on request.

No.
		£	s	d
11. Otter, with tooled pigskin top and pigskin tassels		3	5	0
12. Otter, with head		3	10	0
13. Sealskin, with tooled pigskin top and pigskin tassels		2	16	0
14. Brown Buckskin, with brass opening top		4	18	6
15. Pigskin, with antique brass opening top		6	6	0
16. "Hunting" pattern, pigskin with opening top and silver studs		4	0	0
The same with brass studs		3	15	0
17. Pigskin, with opening top and no studs		3	8	6
18. Buckskin, with laced top		3	15	0
19. Leather, plain with stud in top		1	16	0
20. "Rob Roy," Calfskin, with laced top		3	5	0
Sporran Straps		0	3	0
Chain Straps		0	7	6

26

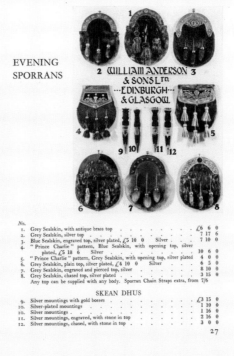

EVENING SPORRANS

No.
		£	s	d
1. Grey Sealskin, with antique brass top		6	6	0
2. Grey Sealskin, silver top		7	17	6
3. Blue Sealskin, engraved top, silver plated, £5 10 0 Silver		7	10	0
4. "Prince Charlie" pattern, Blue Sealskin, with opening top, silver plated, £5 18 6 Silver		10	6	0
5. "Prince Charlie" pattern, Grey Sealskin, with opening top, silver plated		4	0	0
6. Grey Sealskin, plain top, silver plated, £4 10 0 Silver		6	5	0
7. Grey Sealskin, engraved and pierced top, silver		8	10	0
8. Grey Sealskin, chased top, silver plated		3	15	0
Any top can be supplied with any body. Sporran Chain Straps extra, from 7/6				

SKEAN DHUS

		£	s	d
9. Silver mountings with gold bosses		3	15	0
10. Silver-plated mountings		1	10	0
10. Silver mountings		1	16	0
11. Silver mountings, engraved, with stone in top		2	16	0
12. Silver mountings, chased, with stone in top		3	0	0

27

Right:
The Balmoral with diced band.

Bottom Right:
Sgian Dubhs.

the similar informal Tam o'Shanter. The crown of the Balmoral was originally quite voluminous with a tourie, traditionally red, in the centre. The ribbons at the back were originally used to tightly secure the bonnet and a clan badge is worn on the left hand side attached to a silk or grosgrain cockade. Sometimes there is a diced red and white check band round the base of this bonnet.

Sgian Dubh
The name Sgian Dubh is Gaelic for Black Knife and was originally used by the Highlander to defend himself from attack. He also used it for practical purposes such as skinning rabbits, preparing food and meat, or cutting bread or other materials. The Highlander kept his Sgian Dubh concealed under his left armpit.
Later in the 17th and 18th centuries it was

Headwear
Traditionally there are two types of headwear for Highland Dress; the Balmoral and the Glengarry. As with other hats these are not frequently worn today although the Glengarry is by far the most popular form of head dress for Scottish Regiments and pipe bands. The Glengarry was part of the uniform of the Glengarry Fencibles when they were formed in 1784 by Alexander Ronaldson of Donald of Glengarry who is believed to have invented this cap. The Glengarry traditionally has a tourie on top, a rosette cockade on the left and usually ribbons hanging down behind.

The Balmoral came into being early in the 16th century and was subsequently named after Balmoral Castle. It was an alternative to

carried in the upper sleeve or lining of the jacket. When etiquette demanded that concealed weapons had to be revealed when entering the house of a friend, its hiding place gave way to displaying it tucked into the top of the stocking secured by garters.

The Sgian Dubh is now purely ornamental, usually about 7 inches/13cms in length, and worn on the outside of the right leg (or the left leg by the left handed) with about 2 inches/5cms of the upper part visible. Most Sgian Dubhs have a stainless steel blade and a handle made of resin, African black wood or stag horn. The handle is usually ornamented at the top, either with a Celtic design, with stone or stones, or a ball. The scabbard is made of leather or leather substitute and can be ornamented at the top and at the peak with Celtic design on silver or silver plate.

The Kilt Pin

This is purely ornamental and attached to the front apron only, on the right-hand side, quite close to the fringe and about 4 inches/10cms from the bottom of the kilt.

Kilt pins range from a standard blanket pin to ornate pins in sterling silver. They can be a variety of shapes, though mostly sword shapes or bayonet shaped, and they can have Celtic and zoomorphic designs on the blade and Celtic or thistle designs at the top.

Garter Flashes

Garter flashes originated to secure the Sgian Dubh when it was tucked into the kilt hose; they are now an integral part of the outfit but purely ornamental and can be plain coloured or made in the same tartan as the kilt. The elastic of the flashes is hidden underneath the hose turnover, allowing the flashes to be seen on the outside of the leg.

Ties

Kinloch Anderson will recommend that you wear a plain coloured or club tie with the kilt for day or semi-formal occasions but never a tartan tie! A black bow tie is considered correct for eveningwear, although plain coloured cravats are now popular both for daytime occasions such as weddings and also for evening events. A white bow tie is not worn with Highland Dress as it has always been considered to infer that you are a Jacobite.

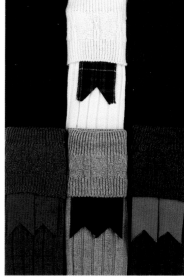

Top Left:
Diced Glengarry in Lovat Green

Above:
Garter Flashes

Below:
Kilt Pins

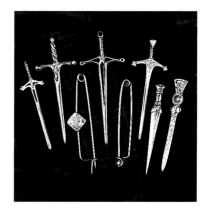

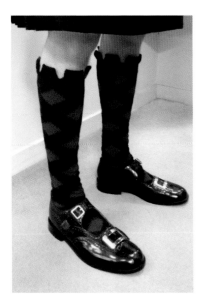

Above:
Castellated kilt hose

Right:
Tartan kilt hose with Ghillie Brogues

Far Right:
Tartan kilt hose with buckle brogues

Ghillie Brogues (shoes)

Highland Dress shoes were originally sandals or brogues made from hide and sometimes elaborately tooled. Today, standard black or brown brogues are correct for daywear. The buckled shoes worn by Chiefs and Chieftains in the 17th and 18th Century have now evolved to become the Buckle Brogues of today worn for dancing and eveningwear. Ghillie Brogues were originally thick soled shoes with no tongues, so that the wearer's feet could dry more quickly in Scotland's wet weather. They have long laces which were wrapped around and tied above the wearer's ankles so that the shoes didn't get pulled off in the mud. Today, Ghillie Brogues are traditionally worn with a formal outfit and the long laces are first twisted four times at the front at ankle level then taken behind with a single twist before tying at the front; the laces remain just above the ankle and are not taken up the leg. The Ghillie Brogue is named after the "Ghillie" the traditional gamekeeper.

Kilt Hose

Kilt Hose were formally fashioned from a piece of tartan fabric cut and sewn in the shape of a stocking. The production of knitted hose arose late in the 18th century, rapidly becoming popular thereafter. Self-coloured kilt hose are now manufactured in bulk alongside other knitted socks. Specially knitted tartan kilt hose remain a highly skilled craft industry, each pair of hose being individually hand-knitted with matching yarn colours. Diced hose, specially knitted in two colours to tone, are chosen by some as a compromise choice.

Castellated top hose, are now rare, and kilt hose today are worn with a turnover at the top and the flashes showing beneath. Most importantly, the top of the hose should be about 3 inches below the knee. The kilt and the hose should never meet!

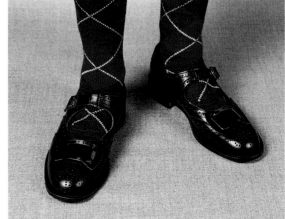

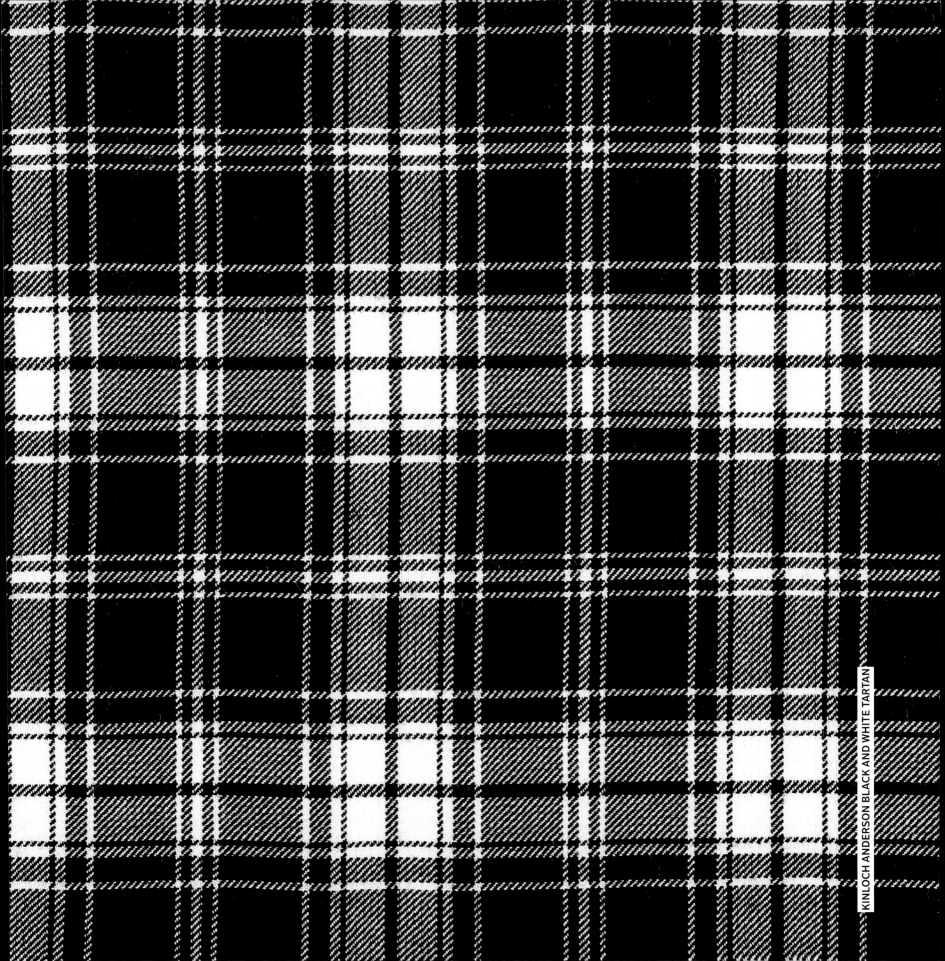

KINLOCH ANDERSON BLACK AND WHITE TARTAN

Making the Kilt

I f wearing the kilt is essentially your responsibility, making the kilt is certainly ours. Kinloch Anderson believes that the Scottish National Dress is the finest National Dress in the world and the Company has been at the forefront of the evolution of kiltmaking and Highland Dress for 145 years, maintaining the best traditions of the past with modern methods of the present.

> *" Production of Highland Dress is indeed a thing apart*
> *from ordinary tailoring involving as it does, a knowledge*
> *both of military and traditional civilian practice*
> *and we make the serious claim that from no firm in Scotland*
> *or elsewhere can you obtain correct Highland Dress*
> *of a style and quality comparable to that which we supply. "*

The Scottish National Dress 5th edition

Above:
Measuring the kilt from beneath the rib cage to the top of the knee.

Left:
A Kinloch Anderson kiltmaker in the Leith Production Unit, Edinburgh.

Kinloch Anderson prides itself on making top quality kilts. No short cuts and no compromises are allowed. Making the kilt is a highly skilled process and requires a great deal of time. An accomplished kiltmaker normally takes about 8 hours to make one kilt. A kilt has no hem and therefore the cloth at the bottom of the kilt cannot be cut as it would fray. The only way to shorten the kilt therefore is to take it apart and shorten it from the waist at the top. The bottom edge of the kilt uses the selvedge edge of the cloth – and indeed it needs to be a special selvedge without showing any mixture of threads; that is why single width cloth of approximately 75 cms is traditionally used. Today double width cloth of 150 cms width is frequently cut down the middle so that both outside selvedge edges are then used in this way.

One man's kilt normally requires 8 yards of fabric but can be even more. The Kinloch Anderson standard kilt has between 23 and 43 pleats each of which is hand deep. The number of pleats depends largely on the size of the pattern repeat of the tartan and there could be as many as 70 pleats in an extra, extra large kilt!

The steps in kiltmaking begin with the chalking process which is the most crucial part of making a kilt. It is a highly skilled procedure to ensure that the tartan sett is perfectly matched throughout. Once chalked onto the cloth the pleats are pinned into place and then hand stitched into the kilt. The pleat size for hip and waist measurements is then

Right: The Kinloch Anderson Operations Manager checking the waistband measurements.

checked to correspond with the customer's measurements.

When the pleating process is complete the excess cloth is cut out of the back so that the kilt is not too bulky round the waist. The cloth off cuts are often used to make belt loops and to attach the buckles onto the kilt.

The next stage is to steam press the pleats into place. Stay tape is then attached to the waist of the kilt so that the waist does not stretch when worn. Tape is also attached round the strap holes to avoid wear and tear at this point. The canvas is then attached for cover, strength and fit. Then the buckles are attached and the belt loops are sewn and matched onto the kilt. Belt loops are only cosmetic and reflect the tradition of hanging the kilt on a tent peg in the battlefield camps of long ago. Next, the waistband needs to be attached and

Chalking the Kilt.

Creating a traditional man's kilt requires knowledge, expertise and painstaking craftsmanship

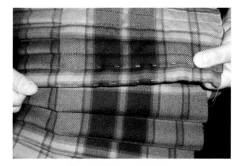

Hand stitching-in pleats.

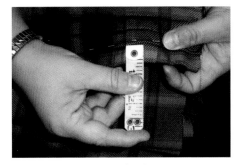

Measuring the pleats.

Cutting away the excess cloth at the back of the kilt to avoid bulk around the waist.

The first hand pressing of the pleats.

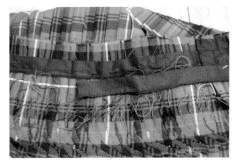

Attaching stay tape to strengthen the kilt at the waist and avoid stretching.

Attaching the buckles with the tartan pattern matched to the kilt.

Attaching the belt loops with the tartan pattern matched to the kilt.

Sewing-in the top cotton lining. The kilt has two linings, first a canvas lining and then a cotton lining to give it a clean finished look.

The final steam press.

Above:
This kilt is depicted by R R Mclan in The Clans of the Scottish Highlands and shows how a box pleated kilt was made in the 18th century.

Top Right:
These kilts are pleated to sett. The tartan sett (pattern) is perfectly matched throughout the kilt.

Right:
A Kinloch Anderson deluxe box pleated kilt.

Far Right:
Line pleated kilts have frequently been chosen by the military and look especially impressive if there is a strong white or yellow line in the sett. Line pleated kilts are still popular today.

the lining is sewn onto the top of the canvas to give a finished look to the inside of the pleats. Finally the pleats, the aprons and the lining of the kilt are all given another meticulous steam press.

The most common way to make the kilt is pleated to sett. This means that visually the tartan sett of the pleats on the back of the kilt is identical to the tartan on the front apron. Alternatively the kilt may be line pleated which gives the back of the kilt a strong lined appearance differing from the tartan sett at the front.

The box pleated kilt was the earliest form of kilt and takes considerable additional skill, experience and time to perfect. The Royal Regiment of Scotland, formed in 2006 wear box pleated kilts in the Government 1A tartan; there is generally a limited demand for the kilt to be made in this way.

KINLOCH ANDERSON ROMANCE TARTAN

Scottish Dress for Ladies

Clothing specifically identified as Scottish was originally in the male domain and indeed Highland Dress remains so today.

However, ladies have made an equally significant contribution to the unique elegance of Scottish clothing throughout the centuries. Towards the end of the 17th century the ancient dress worn by women was called Arisaid. This was a plaid with small stripes. It reached from the neck to the heels and was tied at the lower neck with a buckle of silver or brass, sometimes engraved with animals, sometimes with a centre piece of crystal or fine stones. The plaid itself was loosely pleated and tied with a leather belt which could be adorned at the end with fine stones. The head dress was a piece of linen tightly tied round the head.

Ladies wearing tartan fall into two categories: ladies who wish to wear the tartan associated with their name and their Scottish ancestry, much the same as the man and his kilt – and ladies who love tartan's wonderfully colourful image and who see it as fashionable or perhaps just simply relating to their own personal choice of colour or design.

Manufacturing ladies' skirts was a very significant business for Kinloch Anderson in the 1970s and 1980s. Ladies' classic kilted tartan skirts were then at the height of fashion – particularly in Italy – and the company made over 100,000 skirts a year predominantly for export to European countries – Italy, France, Germany, Austria, Switzerland, Holland, Norway, Sweden and Finland – but also to North America and Japan. In 1979 Kinloch Anderson received the Queen's Award for Export.

Above: The Arisaid as depicted in R R McIan's The Clans of the Scottish Highlands published 1845.

Left: Ladies tartan kilted skirt pictured in 1980s.

Above: Ladies all round pleated tartan skirts in 1980s.

Right: Ladies box pleated tweed and tartan skirts in 1980s.

Left:
The Kinloch Anderson shop in Harrods.

Below:
Ladies tartan kilted skirt in 2000s.

At that time skirts were made not only under the Kinloch Anderson label but also for famous brands including Burberry, Pringle, DAKS, the Scotch House, Ballantyne, Lyle and Scott, Aquascutum and many more. There was a Kinloch Anderson shop on the ground floor of Harrods selling Kinloch Anderson's finest skirts and Scottish clothing.

Ladieswear

The kilted skirt is the most traditional skirt style for ladies. It is a wrap around skirt modelled on the man's kilt but the pleats are not so deep. It is made with a hem and not along the selvedge edge of the cloth and it is easy and comfortable to wear. The lady's kilted skirt is made using the same or lighter wool worsted tartan fabrics than the man's kilt.

It has two straps and buckles and the Kinloch Anderson ladies' kilted skirt has the fringe on the right hand side of the garment in accordance with the man's traditional kilt. The ladies' kilted skirt is very versatile and can be worn at any length from mini to full length.

Other tartan skirt styles made by Kinloch Anderson include the traditional pleated all round skirt, a box pleated skirt with two or three box pleats at the back and front and a straight skirt with or without a single pleat or with open side vents. A more contemporary bias cut skirt and a pleated skirt with cross cut waistband are amongst the alternatives for the younger more fashionable market.

Since earliest times silk has always been a favourite for ladies' skirts and this tradition continues with long full silk skirts for evening wear, elegant straight cut long silk skirts or long silk kilted skirts.

Other ladieswear Scottish clothing items made in tartan or tweed include ladies' trousers, ladies' waistcoats, ladies' jackets, the serape or ladies' cape usually made from tartan in Lambswool, Lamora or Cashmere fabric.

The traditional Highland Dress blouse for ladies is a jabot blouse, but a blouse with a lace mandarin collar and placket is an alternative.

Above:
Ladies mini tartan kilted skirt in 2000s.

Right:
Ladies long tartan silk skirt in 2000s.

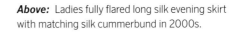

Above: Ladies fully flared long silk evening skirt with matching silk cummerbund in 2000s.

Above:
Ladies silk sash worn over a lace mandarin collar blouse.

Left:
Ladies short pleated skirt with cross cut waistband in 2000s.

1   2   3   4

Above:
Four different methods of tying the ladies sash which depend on traditional practice and custom.

Ladies' Sashes

For several centuries it has been traditional for ladies to wear a Sash with evening dress and it remains most frequently worn for formal Highland Dress Dancing and Highland Dress Balls to accompany the men wearing the kilt. The ladies' Sash may be made from wool or from silk.

These illustrations of ladies wearing the Sash are based upon a careful study of old portraits, prints and traditional practice and bear the authoritative approval of the Lord Lyon King of Arms.

Number 1

This is the most common way to wear the Sash over the right shoulder across the breast and secured by a pin or brooch on the right shoulder.

Number 2

Wives of Clan Chiefs and wives of Colonels of Scottish Regiments wear a fuller Sash over the left shoulder and with a brooch on the left shoulder.

Number 3

This is worn by married ladies who wear the Sash in the Clan tartan of their maiden name. This Sash is worn over the right shoulder and fastened in a large bow.

Number 4

Some country dancers like to wear this Sash which does not cross over the front of the dress but is buttoned at the back of the waist or held by a small belt and is secured at the right shoulder by a pin or brooch.

Early Marketing, Exporting and Brand Development

EARLY MARKETING

It is fortunate that early advertising and marketing record books were made and perhaps more remarkable that two of them from 1868 to 1913 and from 1929 to 1934 are still held in the Company today. They provide a fascinating insight into our forebears' proactive approach to sales with great foresight and dedicated customer service. We should also remind ourselves of the limited technology and therefore the effort and cost required to keep this material and signed copies of letters. If mistakes were made there was no alternative but to type the whole letter again – and certainly no grammatical or spelling checks! The fact that all this information – even the ticket for the William Anderson & Sons Ltd Supper and Dance on Saturday 22nd February 1913 has been carefully kept could perhaps indicate that even then, the family believed in the potential longevity of the Company.

The most frequent stage for a family business to falter as such, is around the third or fourth generation. Yet W J Kinloch Anderson, the fourth generation, adapted production to supply the particular clothing needed during the Second World War when practical, simple, hardwearing clothes were more in demand than finely tailored suits. He understood the importance of servicing the Scottish Regiments and went on trips for many weeks by boat in order to do so. Without television or computers in order to relay global information, he personally travelled to see for himself the potential for the export of Scottish clothing and textiles and essentially opened the door for the fifth generation, Douglas Kinloch Anderson, to take up the challenge.

Above:
Wm Anderson & Sons Ltd. Supper and Dance Ticket 1913.

Left:
George Street , Edinburgh in 1868.

TELEGRAPHIC ADDRESS: "UNIFORMS, EDINBURGH" ___ TELEPHONE №. 77.

Wᴹ. ANDERSON & SONS,
CLOTHIERS &
MILITARY TAILORS.

GLASGOW OFFICE,
196 Sᵀ VINCENT STREET.

14 George Street,
Edinburgh 10th March, 1911.

His Majesty's Coronation

Sir,

We enclose a Coloured Drawing of Deputy Lieutenant Full
Dress Uniform, and should you require such or Levee Dress of
any other kind, we respectfully solicit your enquiries. We
specialise in this class of work, and also the Velvet Court
Dress with cut steel trimmings which is used by Gentlemen
attending Court who have no Special Uniform.

We were never in a better position than now to execute
your orders as our Staff is larger, and our experience much
greater. Our Military business has extended enormously in
the last few years, and we are, therefore, in the most
favourable position in the Markets to buy everything pertaining to Uniform and Accoutrements at the keenest quotations;
our customers thus get the benefit of the highest class productions at extremely moderate prices.

We will be glad to submit estimates for anything you
may require.

We are,

enclo.   Your obedient servants,

W.K.A./J.D.

Wᵐ Anderson & Sons

Right:
Letter respectfully soliciting enquiries
for "our highest class productions at
extremely moderate prices".

WM ANDERSON
& SONS LTD

CLOTHIERS AND
MENS OUTFITTERS .

PRINCIPALS.
WM KINLOCH ANDERSON.
W. HISLOP ANDERSON.
J. T. BELL.

*Glasgow Branch
157 Hope Street.*

14 & 16 George Street.

Edinburgh. 25th Oct. 1929.

Dear Sir,

We understand that you are likely to be
passed out of Sandhurst shortly.

We are the leading Firm in Scotland for
Highland Outfitting and are recognised as OFFICIAL
OUTFITTERS to nearly all the SCOTTISH REGIMENTS.   We
specialise in this class of work, and would be glad to
have the opportunity of submitting an estimate for
Outfit for any Regiment.

If you will kindly complete the enclosed
card and post it to us, we will send you full details.

Arrangements will be made for your being
measured at Sandhurst before you leave, and after
gazetting, fitting would be done in London or elsewhere
to suit your convenience.

Should you decide to place your order with
us, you may rest assured that, with our expert knowledge
of all details pertaining to uniform, everything would
be carried out to your entire satisfaction.

Your obedient servants,

WM. ANDERSON & SONS LTD.

Wm Kinloch Anderson

DIRECTOR.

Left:
Letter to a Sandhurst officer
asking for the opportunity to
submit an estimate for his
next Regimental Outfit.

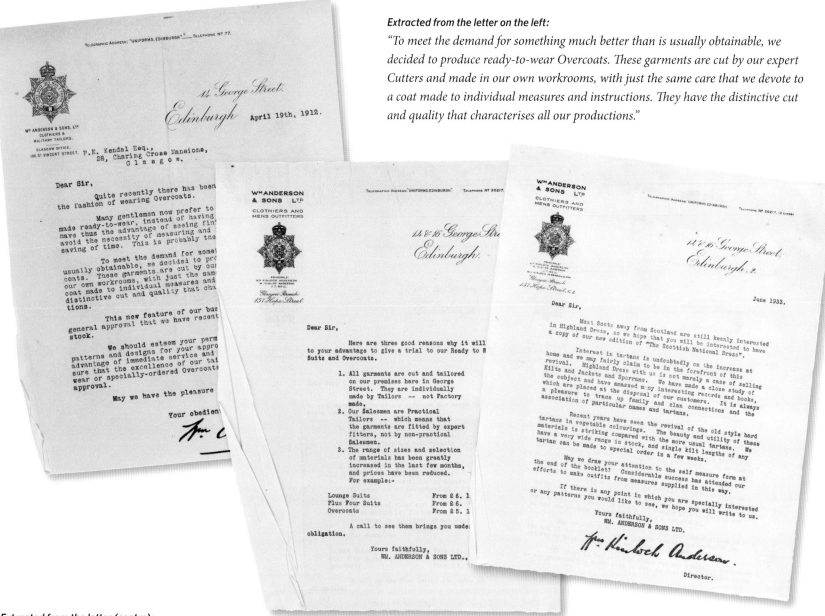

CHRISTMAS
PRESENTS

FOR MEN
OF
ALL AGES

Ties
2/6
to
6/6

A Tie is a present that never goes wrong. A great selection of stripes and spots in all the fashionable colours. If your choice is not approved, we are delighted to make an exchange.

Prices . . 2/6 to 6/6

Gloves
5/6
to
27/6

Any man who has a car will be pleased to have a pair of warm Winter Gloves. Other styles of Gloves to suit every purpose.

Knitted Wool and String Hunting Gloves   5/6
Chamois Gloves 7/6, 10/6
Hogskin Gloves (top left illustration)   11/6, 18/6
Lined Leather Gloves (Lambskin, Leather, and Cashmere)   .   10/6, 15/6, 17/6
Hogskin Gloves, lined Cashmere and Lambskin 23/6, 27/6
Imitation Fur Gloves and Gauntlets.   13/6, 25/6

Scarves
6/9
to
12/6

Spot Foulard Silk (as illustrated), 8/6
Spot Cashmere Wool (as illustrated), 10/6
Evening Silk Mufflers   12/6

Sporting Designs
Checked Shetland Wool (as illustrated below)   6/9

WE ARE ALWAYS WILLING TO SEND GOODS ON APPROVAL
Customers should mention their home address, and new customers when ordering should send cash, or instruct us to send C.O.D.

Handkerchiefs
From
4/6
half-doz.

A box of Linen Handkerchiefs or one or two Silk Handkerchiefs are a very acceptable present. Packed in Attractive Gift

WM. ANDERSON & SONS LTD.
Men's Outfitters
14-16 GEORGE STREET
EDINBURGH, 2

WM. ANDERSON & SONS Ltd.

Above:
Promotional Leaflet 1933

Below:
The Scotsman May 2nd 1931

Copy reads:

ROYAL VISIT IN JULY.
Drawing Room at the Palace of Holyrood House.

LEVEE Dress has been ordered for gentlemen attending this function.

Full dress uniform, either civil or military is correct, but in certain cases Service Dress is permissible. Civilians may wear velvet Court Dress, the alternative Court Dress or Highland Dress.

Wm Anderson & Sons are specialists in making uniforms of all kinds as well as Court and Highland Dress.
Enquiries invited. Estimates on request.

EXPORTING

The Company began exporting on a wholesale basis at the end of the Second World War. A considerable number of Scots had emigrated to Canada and USA and there was a market for Scottish clothing – lambswool, Cashmere and Fair Isle knitwear and accessories – and also for those who wanted the tartan associated with their name, mostly for skirts or kilts. So, one of the Kinloch Anderson export activities was to service this requirement for Scottish Country Dancing, Highland Balls, St Andrews Society events, Highland Games and Burns Nights.

Of course the interesting range of merchandise also appealed to a wider discerning clientele attracted to high quality imports from Scotland. Agents were appointed for North America and Canada and merchandise was sold into Department Stores and a wide range of speciality shops. One of these was Scotland House in Alexandria, Virginia – an import shop specialising in the best of Scottish clothing and textiles including tartans and Highland Dress, and this shop was aquired by Kinloch Anderson in 1978.

In the late 1960s export markets in Europe became increasingly important. The Edinburgh Production Unit in George Street was expanded into additional manufacturing facilities in Tranent (East Lothian), Glasgow and then a new factory in Muirkirk (Ayrshire). These were now mostly making classic ladies' skirts in tweeds and tartans. The Company then built up a wide European customer base in Germany, Italy, France, Switzerland, Holland, Denmark, Norway and Sweden with resident agents in all these countries. Classic skirts were the height of fashion and Kinloch Anderson exhibited regularly at The Salon de la Maille or Prêt-à-Porter clothing exhibitions in Paris and also elsewhere in Europe. Additionally the Kinloch Anderson sales and marketing drive was supported by photography taken in London using top fashion models of the day.

This period was demonstrably successful and the company was making over 100,000 skirts a year. In 1979 Kinloch Anderson won The Queen's Award for Export and in 1980 skirt production moved into a large factory unit in Restalrig in Edinburgh. In recent times Russia has become a market for Kinloch Anderson ladies' skirts similar to those of the European market 35 years previously.

Douglas Kinloch Anderson first went to Japan in 1972. The Japanese appreciate quality clothing and Kinloch Anderson's fine classic Scottish skirts were right for the Japanese market. A resident agent was appointed and the skirts sold so well that a Japanese skirt size chart was produced which is still used today.

Above:
KA wholesale kilts and skirts.

Above and Right:
Top fashion models of the 1970s.

In 2012 Kinloch Anderson partnered with Brooks Brothers in order to open a Highland Dress department
in their flagship store in Madison Avenue, New York. This renewed an earlier connection with Brooks
Brothers with whom the Company had a similar trading arrangement in the 1950s.

Right:
Rugs for USA

Far Right:
Kinloch Anderson merchandise for USA
in the 1970s

BRAND DEVELOPMENT

Examples of
Kinloch Anderson Shops
in the Far East which are
either free standing,
in Shopping Malls or
Concessions in
Department Stores.

BRAND DEVELOPMENT

Business never stands still. Market economies fluctuate and fashions change. The post war era when ladies bought clothing intended to last, began to give way to more fanciful clothing with a faster turnover. Clothing became available at a less expensive price due to imports from the Far East and Eastern Europe, where labour costs were comparatively low.

This was the time when well known international brands started to manufacture their clothing ranges under licence in countries where this could be done more cost effectively. Kinloch Anderson was already exporting to Japan and had many good business contacts in that country. The opportunity to develop the *Kinloch Anderson Brand* under licence was taken.

The first Managing Agent for the *Kinloch Anderson Brand* in Japan was a company called Fukusuke, originally famous for making "tabi" the traditional Japanese socks. This Company had branched out widely into the textile and clothing sector and a number of licensees were appointed for Kinloch Anderson. A significant later development was the appointment of a well known textile and fashion group as menswear licensees for Kinloch Anderson and more than 70 Kinloch Anderson shops and sections were established in major Department Stores across the country.

The marketing effort was supported by frequent visits to Japan, with participation in several British Fairs in well known stores in Tokyo and Osaka and Kinloch Anderson staff demonstrated kiltmaking

and gave lectures on tartan. The British Embassy in Tokyo supported the Company by holding a prestigious promotional event for Kinloch Anderson. A special centenary tartan was designed for the famous Mitsukoshi Department Store Group which is still used to this day.

In the early 1990s the next market in Asia to be tackled was Taiwan where the initial introduction to the market was through a Trade Mission. The first licensee was a household textiles company which demonstrated the potential of Kinloch Anderson as a "lifestyle" brand not confined to clothing and fashion. A Managing Agent and licensees were soon appointed in the key clothing areas and some 15 product categories were established including successful developments in childrenswear and young ladies' fashion. There are well over 100 Kinloch Anderson shops in Taiwan and it is not uncommon to find 4 or 5 Kinloch Anderson Shops in one Department Store. As in Japan, the growth of the business was supported by frequent visits and events including lectures and presentations to organisations and trade groups including the External Trade Development Council, (CETRA) in Taiwan. Brand awareness was also enhanced by striking advertisements on some 75 buses in Taipei.

Korea is a sophisticated consumer market with some of the finest Department Stores in the world. In the 1990s Kinloch Anderson were fortunate to find excellent licensee partners in menswear who have continued to develop, not only the *Kinloch Anderson Brand* but also two subsidiary brands *Kinloch by Kinloch Anderson* for leisure and casualwear and *Kinloch2* targeted at the fashion

A selection of Kinloch Anderson merchandise made under licence overseas includes men's and ladies' shoes, leathergoods, children's shoes, young ladieswear, formal menswear, household textiles, childrenswear and men's casualwear.

Above Left: A Kinloch Anderson Licensees Conference, Tokyo June 2008. ***Above Right:*** The Kinloch Anderson Stand at the Beijing CHIC International Exhibition 26th-29th March 2013.

Above: At the British Embassy in Tokyo with Japanese Licensees, June 2008.

conscious younger men's market. This success in the menswear field has been added to by the development of men's and ladies' shoes which have achieved substantial coverage in the Korean market.

Mainland China is a challenging market but Kinloch Anderson has taken up this challenge as China is on course to be the largest luxury goods market in the world. After a difficult start with trademark issues, including shops pirating the Kinloch Anderson brand name, good progress is now being made with the establishment of a growing number of men's outerwear and underwear shops.

A key decision was to appoint a member of the sixth generation Peter Kinloch Anderson as Brand Development Director based in Shanghai and therefore available to travel easily throughout China and other Asian countries. There are also a number of development projects outwith the clothing industry including the marketing of the exclusive Kinloch Anderson whisky range which enhances the Brand image of "British Lifestyle – Scottish Character".

Left:
Kinloch Anderson Shoe Collection Fashion Event, Korea 2006.

Below:
Advertising on buses in Taipei 2006.

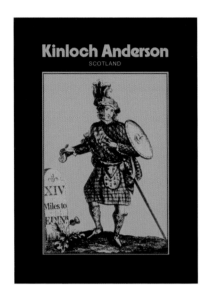

The Kinloch Anderson brand image makes a major contribution to the awareness and marketing of the Company in Asian and other markets. The Kinloch Anderson identity is founded on the history and heritage of a six generation family owned Company and is enhanced by the granting of three Royal Warrants. The brand reflects not only the best of British Style and Fashion but also the lifestyle of Scotland.

The unique specially designed Kinloch Anderson tartans and House Check have been widely used and the Kinloch Anderson Thistle and Highlander emblems have achieved increasing recognition. There is also a growing trend toward supporting the ranges produced under licence with complementary products made in Scotland and the UK, as these emphasise the authenticity and integrity of the Brand.

Perhaps the most important factor of all has been the substantial and sustained effort made by the family Directors and senior staff. Every year frequent overseas visits have been made in order to understand the needs of markets and to establish lasting relationships with the customers, agents and licensee partners.

Kinloch Anderson

SCOTLAND

Above:
The Kinloch Anderson Highlander logo

Centre:
The KA Thistle logo

Right:
The lifestyle of Scotland –
The High Constables of the City of Edinburgh take the Salute at the Royal Edinburgh Military Tattoo 2011 (Deirdre Kinloch Anderson fourth from the left in the front line).

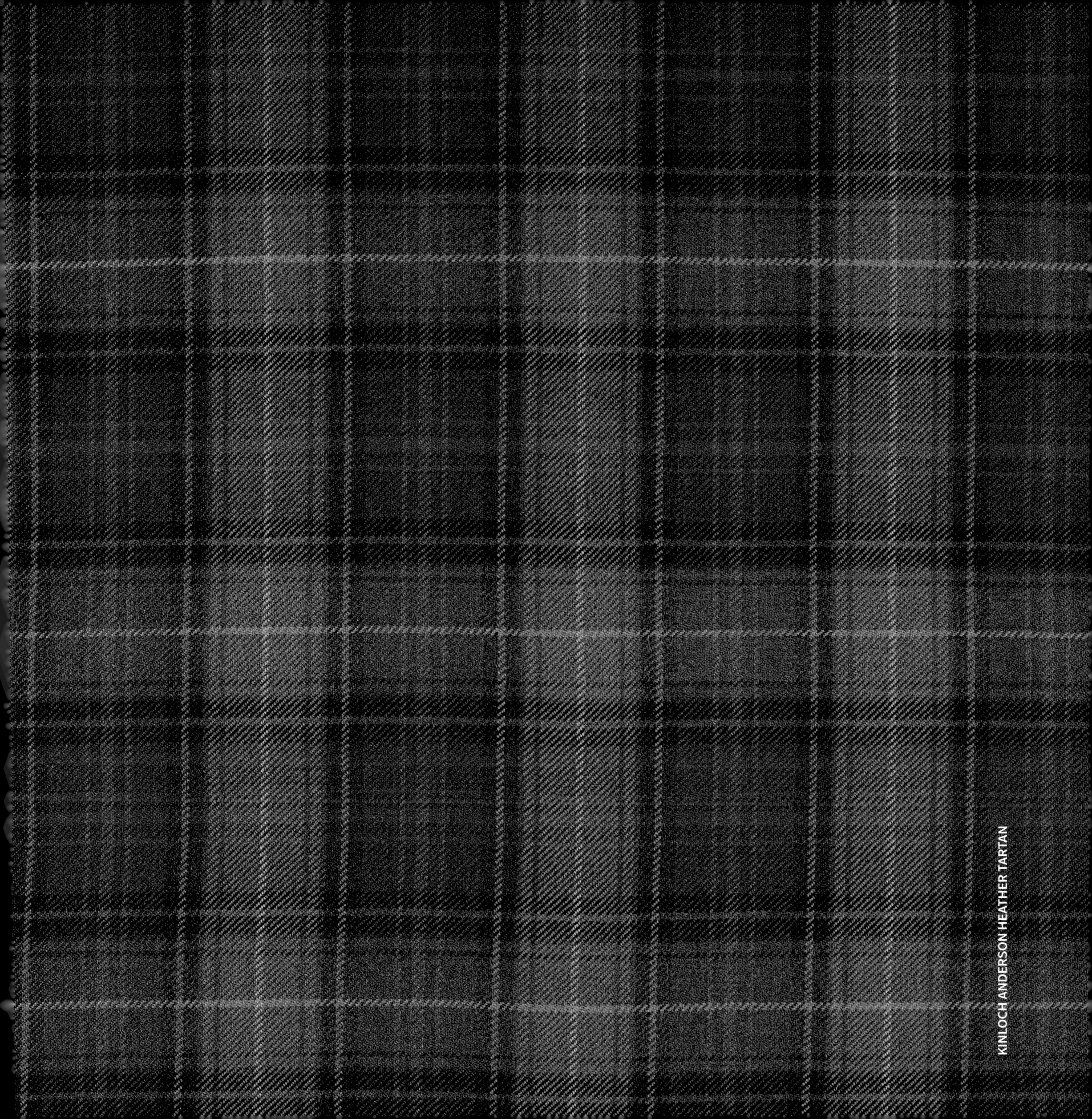

KINLOCH ANDERSON HEATHER TARTAN

The Global Impact of Tartan

Tartan is a great cultural icon for Scotland and a national mark of identification recognised worldwide. Perhaps no other country can boast such a strong image. It proclaims the geographical or spiritual roots of its global family of descendants in North America, New Zealand, Australia, South Africa and many more countries besides to a total of over 50 million people.

As Scottish culture has evolved, tartan has evolved alongside it. Tartan has, and will continue, to defeat scientific precision as to an agreed date of origin. Some say it originated in 1200 BC in China as found on Caucasian Mummies in the Chinese Desert, others that it was first worn by Celts who came from South Russia to the Western Seaboard. In Scotland checked cloths have indeed been excavated from burial sites back in 300AD. However, the first written mention of tartan was in 1538 when "Heland tartane" (Highland tartan) occurred in an account of clothes for King James V. The word "héland" (highland) clearly relates to Scotland. The design would probably not have looked like tartan as we know it today but rather some checked and striped fabric woven in natural and vegetable dyed wools – in this case for a pair of close fitting tights.

Left:
In the 19th century Kinloch Anderson kept tartan books to number and record every customer's order.

Right:
A catwalk day outfit featuring a Buchanan tartan kilt and a tweed day jacket and waistcoat.

Bottom Right:
Silk dress in the Buchanan tartan
On the Catwalk of the Coronation Festival held in Buckingham Palace Gardens July 2013.

Clanship was the social system of Scotland. The essential link was between the Chief and the people of the Clan and the clan tartan came to be associated with the dominant clan or family. At that time other tartan setts were district setts and related to a particular geographic district irrespective of name and this was usually an area of around 50 square miles.

During the 16th century evidence for tartan became more plentiful. The word itself was derived from the French word "Tartaine" and the Gaelic word was "Breacan". It was not until the late 17th or early 18th century that tartan was adopted by families, clans or districts, to which a particular pattern or sett gave a sense of belonging.

Tartan has always been the most distinctive element of Highland Dress, indeed the two are inextricably linked. Highland Dress was so named because it was in the Highlands and Islands that it flourished long before it was worn by the Lowland Scots.

Left:
A catwalk evening outfit featuring a silk Montrose jacket in MacBeth tartan and a Royal Stewart tartan kilt with a dress horsehair sporran

Bottom Left:
Long flared silk skirt in the Royal Warrant Holders Association tartan with a Celtic brooch worn at the neck
On the Catwalk of the Coronation Festival held in Buckingham Palace Gardens July 2013

To this very day when you see tartan you immediately think of Scotland. Just as Scots people ventured overseas so has tartan spread its wings and there are now new commemorative tartans, corporate tartans, overseas tartans, name tartans, fashion tartans and many more. Tartan is a huge success story, not only for Highland Dress but it also graces the catwalks of Scotland, London, Paris, Milan, New York and many more worldwide.

Family Tartan Design

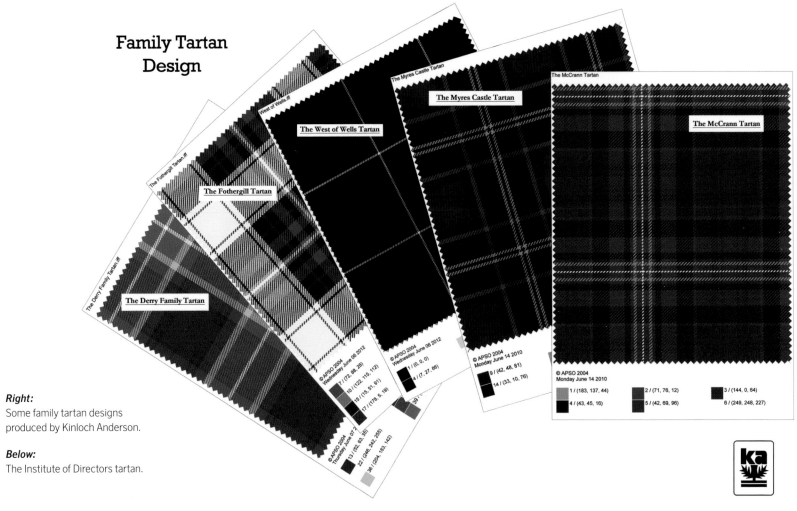

The Derry Family Tartan
The Fothergill Tartan
The West of Wells Tartan
The Myres Castle Tartan
The McCrann Tartan

Right:
Some family tartan designs
produced by Kinloch Anderson.

Below:
The Institute of Directors tartan.

Tartan Design

The heritage and history of tartan is a long and fascinating story beyond the remit of this book. However, tartan is a living medium for expressing identity and it is a specialist activity of Kinloch Anderson to respond to individuals, organisations and corporate bodies who wish to express their image with their own exclusively designed tartan. Kinloch Anderson designs a new tartan from concept right through to the manufacture and the supply of exclusive clothing, gifts and accessories.

Kinloch Anderson
SCOTLAND

EDINBURGH ZOO
PANDAS

Launch of the Club's own tartan
Kinloch Anderson has designed the Club's official tartan, based on the sett of the Clan Campbell after the founder of the Club, Neville Campbell. The colour influences include the saltire and the Club's crest. Full story on pg 2.

Edinburgh Zoo Panda Tartan
Exclusively designed by Kinloch Anderson,

DRAMBUIE

Far Left:
The Edinburgh Zoo Panda tartan.

Top Right:
The Caledonian Club (London) tartan.

Left:
The Drambuie tartan.

The Kinloch Anderson Procedure for Tartan Design

Tartan is a gift that Scotland has given to the world and Kinloch Anderson takes great pride and pleasure in responding to the expressed wish of customers wanting to have an exclusively designed tartan. Wherever possible great importance is placed on any historic background and association with Scotland usually regarding a name or a location.

Tartan belongs to Scottish culture. It is a design with a meaning, a personal significance, a sense of belonging and a special relevance. Tartan is very much more than a check design with several colours of vertical and horizontal lines. Tartan's heritage lies associated with the woven fabric, with Scotland's National Dress, the kilt and other items of clothing, accessories, furnishings and gifts.

When creating a tartan, designs are initially produced onto

paper with a variety of options to be considered. As early as possible the intended use for the tartan is discussed so that the most suitable fabric can be recommended. This also means that the yarn colours nearest to the colours of the design can be shown for approval prior to the tartan being woven.

Right:
Woven labels for corporate customers.

An important aspect of this service is to advise on the minimum quantity weave or the minimum number of items for each particular product. Orders are purchased in the normal way but Kinloch Anderson will hold in stock any excess fabric for future use and products subsequently made from it are then charged as a make up charge only. This has proved to be a flexible and effective way of working.

An additional enhancement to the exclusive tartan merchandise is to have woven labels attached to the garment giving the name of the tartan, together with the Kinloch Anderson name and wording such as "Exclusively designed in Scotland". Also a swing ticket telling the background story to the tartan and showing company names and logos adds interest to the product.

The customer is asked to plan the design project well in advance as the design process takes time to complete. 8–10 weeks is often required for the weaving process and time should also be generously allowed to make the products thereafter. The final recommendation is that the tartan is registered in the Scottish Register of Tartans, the official record of all publicly known tartans. Following the registration process a fine Certificate of Registration is provided, signed by the Keeper of the Register. If copyright is required, however, this needs to be done separately.

THE KINLOCH ANDERSON TARTANS

Kinloch Anderson has designed and developed 9 exclusive tartans to comprise the *Kinloch Anderson Tartan Collection*. All of the tartans are based on the Clan Anderson tartan sett thereby reflecting the heritage of the Anderson family's ownership and management of the Company over six generations. The tartans are used for Kinloch Anderson customers at home and overseas for the supply of items of clothing and accessories as they promote the *Kinloch Anderson Brand*. The tartans have been woven into medium and light weight pure wool worsted fabrics and also into fine Dupion silk.

The Kinloch Anderson Tartan - The name "Anderson" means the son of Andrew and Kinloch means head of the loch. In this tartan there are 3 parallel burgundy coloured lines with the central line wider than those on either side and this is a feature taken from the Clan Anderson tartan. The colours of the tartan are rich classic and timeless and have been chosen to reflect the Kinloch Anderson lifestyle – they are navy, border brown, 2 shades of burgundy, black and antique gold.

The Kinloch Anderson Hunting Tartan – follows the tradition of hunting tartans which reflect the darker shades of green and brown to be seen in the Scottish landscape as well as the pursuit of activities such as hunting and shooting. The colours of this tartan are tartan green, blue, burgundy, black and light beige.

The Kinloch Anderson Dress Tartan – introduces white which is a characteristic of many dress tartans. The other colours are navy, 2 shades of burgundy, moss green, cream and black.

The Romance of Kinloch Anderson Tartan - introduces some softer more feminine shades in order to appeal to children and ladies and also to be suitable to wear in Spring and Summer. The colours of the tartan are pink, sky blue, light green and 3 shades of purple.

The Kinloch Anderson Thistle Tartan - introduces rich deep purple and green hues which are found in the thistle, the emblem and flower of Scotland. The colours are 2 shades of dark purple, dark green, turquoise blue, dark burgundy and dark charcoal. The Kinloch Anderson Thistle is also a key trade mark of the Company.

The Kinloch Anderson Castle Grey Tartan – essentially incorporates 4 shades of grey with a red and white overcheck. The grey colours evoke the grey stone of the Castles of Scotland in particular the famous Castle in the heart of Edinburgh, the home of Kinloch Anderson.

The Kinloch Anderson Heather Tartan - introduces a special mixture of two purple heather colours which pervade the Scottish landscape in Autumn, together with 3 shades of green and soft grey all of which reflect Scotland's hills.

TARTAN OR CHECK –
WHAT'S THE DIFFERENCE?

There is no definitive answer as they have been closely linked and frequently interchanged.

Some special qualities of tartan are:

- Tartan belongs to cultural tradition
- Tartan has a symbolic meaning usually with a background story
- The longevity of tartan identity passes from one generation to the next
- Tartan inspires feelings of belonging and fosters loyalty to its owner and cultural origin
- Historically most tartans were associated with particular families or clans or geographic districts of Scotland
- New tartans evolve today and continue to maintain cultural traditions and symbolic values
- The Scottish Register of Tartans is maintained by the National Records of Scotland as the official database for all past recorded tartans and for new tartans which meet its criteria for registration.

The Kinloch Anderson Rowanberry – introduces 4 shades of red and a golden yellow overcheck. In Scotland the Rowan Tree's berries are red whereas in Asia there are some species where they are a golden yellow. This tree is famed for its hardiness and ability to survive in the mountains as well as its long and interesting history and mythology. In Scotland it is called rudha-an, meaning 'red one'.

The Kinloch Anderson House Check is a fashion check in classic shades of camel, cream, navy and brown which give it a versatile and sophisticated look.

The Kinloch Anderson Black and White Tartan – was designed because black and white is so universally popular, so distinctive and so easy to wear. Black and white colours always remain both traditional and contemporary and therefore chosen by Kinloch Anderson to be included in their Tartan Collection.

THE KINLOCH ANDERSON HOUSE CHECK

The Kinloch Anderson House Check.
In addition to the 9 Kinloch Anderson tartans, Kinloch Anderson also has its own exclusive House Check. The Kinloch Anderson House Check is a fashion check of more simple design which has been widely used for many of Kinloch Anderson's ranges of clothing and products.

The Kinloch Anderson Tartan Collection

THE BALMORAL TARTAN

The sense of belonging that accompanies tartan can be very strong. In history, many conflicts have arisen over tartan and strong views regarding tartan ownership still exist today.

There are universal tartans for everyone to wear and similarly a large number of popular tartans are without any restrictions. Other tartans, however, are exclusive and restricted to the use of their owners, none more so than the Balmoral tartan.

The Balmoral tartan is the private property of the Reigning Monarch of Great Britain; other members of the Royal Family may only wear it in accordance with the Sovereign's wishes.

Above: The Balmoral tartan includes unusual twisted yarns composed of different ratios of black and white threads reflecting the granite stone which is typical of the Deeside area including Balmoral Castle itself.

Below:
Balmoral Castle, Deeside, Scotland.

The Balmoral tartan was designed in 1857 by HRH Prince Albert, Prince Consort to HM Queen Victoria and was named after their Castle and Estate in Deeside in Scotland. The young Queen Victoria paid her first visit to Scotland in 1842. She fell in love with tartan at a time when there was a growing passion for Scottish Clans, Scottish tartans and the Highlands of Scotland.

Kinloch Anderson have tailored garments in the Balmoral tartan over many years. The Sovereign's Piper is the only person outside the Royal Family who is authorised to wear the Balmoral Tartan and Kinloch Anderson has a long tradition of supplying Highland Dress outfits to Pipers of the Sovereign.

Below:
Pipe Major Brian McRae,
(Gordon Highlanders)
The Sovereign's Piper 1980 – 1995.

Right:
Pipe Major Alastair Cuthbertson,
(1st Battalion , The Royal Scots)
The Sovereign's Piper 2006 – 2008.

Centre:
Pipe Major Derek Potter RVM,
(Royal Scots Dragoon Guards)
The Sovereign's Piper 2008 – 2012.

The position of the Sovereign's Piper
is one of the highest accolades available
to a piper serving in the Armed Forces.

THE SCOTTISH REGISTER OF TARTANS

Until February 2009 all recording and registration of tartan had been carried out by privately owned societies or companies and there was no definitive national record of tartans of official standing. Historic artefacts were free to be sold overseas, protection for the avoidance of fraudulent claims was unavailable and the standing and status of tartan was at risk.

The advent of the Scottish Parliament in Holyrood provided the opportunity to pass a Bill through the Scottish Parliament to establish a national Scottish Register of Tartans to be held in the public domain, safeguarding our tartan heritage in perpetuity.

The initial meeting of representative parties both from within and outwith the tartan industry was convened by Deirdre Kinloch Anderson and held in the Kinloch Anderson Heritage Room on the 26th March 2001. The project included a Parliamentary Consultation Process and Economic Assessment on the value of tartan to Scotland. It engendered huge support but was not without controversy. On several occasions it barely survived, as when, at the time of the parliamentary election in June 2007 the Labour 'champion' lost his seat.

The Tartan Register Bill was taken up as a cross-party example of how all political parties in Scotland could work together. However, it was not until 26th November 2009 that The *Scottish Register Of Tartans* Bill received Royal Assent.

The aim of the Register is to be a natural repository of tartans that is independent, definitive, accessible and sustainable for the promotion and preservation of tartan. The Register also aims to help increase interest in tartan, tourism and general genealogical research. The Register is an official reference and registration source for tartans. Access to it is essentially electronic.

The Register is operated by National Records of Scotland (formerly National Archives of Scotland). The Chief Executive of National Records of Scotland is Keeper of the Records of Scotland and Keeper of the *Scottish Register Of Tartans*. For registration purposes, the definition of tartan is 'a design which is capable of being woven, consisting of two or more alternating coloured stripes which combine vertically and horizontally to form a repeated check pattern'. When applying for registration the new tartan must be unique to the Register, such that, neither the name nor the design can be confused with any tartan already recorded.

Anyone can submit an application to register a tartan in the Register. The registration request is reviewed and checked against the registration criteria. The applicant is asked to provide a name and address, a photograph or colour image of the tartan design, a description including the colours, thread-count and sett (pattern), the name of the tartan and an association with that name. The applicant is recommended to submit the tartan for registration before having it woven and after registration is then strongly encouraged to have the tartan woven and to send a sample for permanent preservation in the National Archives of Scotland.

Tartan has evolved as part of our culture and must continue to evolve likewise. Many people wanted and indeed thought that the official nature of the new Register would also be judgemental, making rules that would somehow eliminate what is generally referred to as "tartan tat". However, the Holyrood Parliament was clear that it wanted the new legislation to be as inclusive as possible and avoided any aesthetic restrictions on what could be registered.

The Register has a classification system which separates the original clan and family tartans from other categories such as commemorative tartans, military tartans, fashion tartans, name tartans and many others. Interestingly, despite the abundance of cheap tartan souvenirs, tartan itself maintains its dignity and its key role at the top end of the nation's textile industry. If a famous fashion brand introduces a new line of merchandise exclusively sold through its own top-end outlets and this is then subsequently copied into the mass market stores, (albeit in modified form), that line is no longer saleable to the high end customer. Yet tartan is so strong that despite all the tartan fakes and images, tartan has held its profile, is the envy of the world and remains a proud icon of Scotland.

The Scottish Register of Tartans

This is to certify that the following tartan has met the conditions of registration set out in the Scottish Register of Tartans Act, 2008.

Scottish Register of Tartans

Registration Number: 10,000

Thread count details

K/5 M3 LT6 M3 K23 DT2 K2 DT28 T2 DT28 M2 DT2 M7 N4 M/12
(half sett with full pivots)

Colour Details

DT=DARK TAN; T=TAN; LT=LIGHT TAN; K=BLACK; M=MAROON; N=NEUTRAL

George P. MacVou

Keeper of the Scottish Register of Tartans
5 February 2009

THE NATIONAL ARCHIVES OF SCOTLAND
DEFINING MOMENTS IN HISTORY

 The Scottish Government

Above:
The Scottish Highland Dancers at the Edinburgh Military Tattoo wearing skirts sponsored by Kinloch Anderson, provide a magnificent tartan spectacle.

Right:
The Renaissance Club, East Lothian, Scotland, features its own exclusive tartan carpet in the locker room.

Far Right:
A Japanese Kimono with a touch of tartan.

Right:
St Andrews University tartan collection.

THE TARTAN INDUSTRY

The tartan industry is a very significant contributor to the overall Scottish economy equivalent to 5% of national GDP with estimated direct employment of over 4,000 jobs, approximately 1 in every 200 jobs. Tartan has a role to play in the tourist industry, Scottish promotional industry, the textile weaving industry, the knitwear industry, the carpet and furnishing industry, the toy industry, the jewellery industry, the paper and printing industry, the craft industry and not least Scotland's education industry. Whenever and wherever full Highland Dress is worn formally or simply the kilt worn with a shirt or sweater it "steals the show". Such a colourful garment which is worn to just above the knee, is full of movement and swings to the walk let alone to the dance, and makes any man who wears it hold his head high and feel so proud. The National Dress of Scotland is the finest national dress in the world.

Above:
The Commonwealth Games tartan designed by Kinloch Anderson worn by Team Scotland in Melbourne 2006.

Above Left:
The City of Edinburgh tartan designed by Kinloch Anderson and worn by the crew of the Edinburgh Yacht for the Clipper Round the World Yacht Race 2011–12.

Left:
Kinloch Anderson kilt outfits "steal the show" on the catwalk at the Coronation Festival in Buckingham Palace Gardens July 2013.

THE HERITAGE ROOM

Kinloch Anderson

This shows an 8-yard length of Clan Anderson tartan fabric – the amount used to make one man's kilt.

KINLOCH ANDERSON DRESS TARTAN

EXPERTS IN TARTAN SINCE 1868

The Kinloch Anderson Company is proud of its long history and heritage and of continuing to this day to be an independent family run Company

This is a copy of the original partnership agreement which established the company in 1868

Kinloch Anderson was founded in 1868 when William Anderson, an experienced tailor's cutter, started the business with his two sons. The company has evolved over the years from becoming the famous military and civilian tailors and kiltmakers, William Anderson & Sons Ltd, to a period as premier Men's and Ladies Outfitters and then to the development of Kinloch Anderson Ltd as manufacturers of high quality clothing exported to many parts of the world.

Today, the Kinloch Anderson brand name stands for *"The best of British styling and fashion with a Scottish emphasis"* or *"British Style - Scottish Character".*

Six Generations of the Kinloch Anderson family

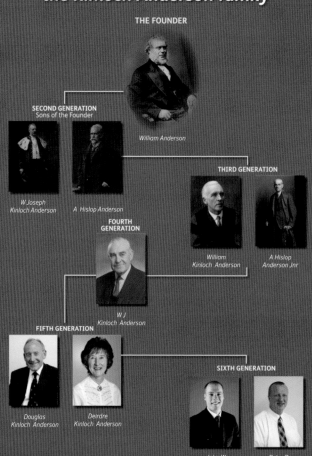

THE FOUNDER

William Anderson

SECOND GENERATION
Sons of the Founder

W Joseph Kinloch Anderson

A Hislop Anderson

THIRD GENERATION

William Kinloch Anderson

A Hislop Anderson Jnr

FOURTH GENERATION

W J Kinloch Anderson

FIFTH GENERATION

Douglas Kinloch Anderson

Deirdre Kinloch Anderson

SIXTH GENERATION

John W Kinloch Anderson

Peter D Kinloch Anderson

The Kinloch Anderson Heritage Room

A WALK ROUND THE HERITAGE ROOM

The Kinloch Anderson Heritage Room opens off the main shop in Leith. It records the 145 year history of the Company and illustrates the story of the development of Highland Dress and tartan clothing told in preceding chapters.

In the shop itself, above the walnut fireplace brought from the George Street premises from which the Company moved in 1980, are framed the tartans worn by the Royal Family. In the centre is a bronze cast of the Royal Warrant of Appointment to His Majesty King George VI above the three current Royal Warrants from Her Majesty The Queen, His Royal Highness The Duke of Edinburgh and His Royal Highness The Prince of Wales.

ENTRANCE PANEL

As you enter, the first display is on the left and reads "Kinloch Anderson since 1868". "The Kinloch Anderson Company is proud of its long history and heritage and of continuing to this day to be an independent family run company". There is a framed copy of the original Partnership Agreement which established the company in 1868 beneath which is written "The Company has evolved over the years from becoming the famous Military and Civilian Tailors and Kiltmakers, William Anderson & Sons Limited, to a period as premier men's and ladies' Outfitters and then to the development of Kinloch Anderson Limited as manufacturers of high quality clothing exported to many parts of the world. Today the *Kinloch Anderson Brand* name stands for "The Best of British Styling and Fashion with a Scottish Emphasis" or "British Style – Scottish Character".

Beside this are the six generations of the Kinloch Anderson family individually photographed and named in family tree format.

Above:
Heritage Room Entrance.

Left:
Six generations of the Kinloch Anderson family.

Showcase 1 : TARTAN HERITAGE

The first Showcase is entitled "Tartan Heritage". A short explanation of tartan is on the wall and reads as follows:

"Tartan is a symbol of kinship and belonging for Scots throughout the world and its simplicity and striking design make it instantly recognisable and infinitely adaptable. There are many examples of checked cloth, similar to tartan, dating far back in antiquity and from many parts of the world. However, Scottish Tartan is generally considered to have developed from the 16th Century onwards. Original checked patterns were woven using vegetable dyes and the patterns formed were known as "setts". These developed into the Clan Tartans we know today.

Following the Battle of Culloden, the wearing of Tartan was outlawed with the intention of destroying the Highland Clan system. The 'Dress Act' was part of the Act of Proscription which came into force on 1 August 1746 and made wearing "the Highland Dress", including tartan or a kilt, illegal in Scotland. The law was repealed in 1782. However, Tartan was still produced and worn by the upper classes and some lowland Scots. Then in 1822 King George IV visited Edinburgh and wore Highland Dress specially made for the occasion. As part of the Pageant, the Highland Chiefs were encouraged to wear their Clan tartans and families who had never been associated with a tartan wanted to have their own. The important outcome of George IV's visit was that it gave the royal seal of approval to Highland Dress. The romanticism of Tartan in Sir Walter Scott's novels and Queen Victoria's love of Highland Dress helped to continue the popularity of tartan through the 19th Century.

During the 20th Century, tartan continued to be worn as both Highland Dress and also increasingly in both classic and high fashion clothing for men and ladies. Recent trends have seen an ever greater popularity of Highland Dress for young men for weddings, formal events and as casual leisurewear."

Two of the most valuable items in this Museum are on display in this Showcase. The first is a pure silk velvet Doublet which was tailored from velvet woven in France, and was first worn in 1822 during King George IV's historic visit to Scotland – the first British Monarch to travel North of the Border, since Charles II departure in 1651. Below this Doublet is a print which shows the Scottish regalia being carried in procession from Edinburgh Castle in 1822 during George IV's visit. The Clan Gathering called to celebrate his visit heralded the rebirth of the wearing of tartan, and the launching of modern Highland Dress. The second is a Royal Company of Archers outfit in muted shades of blue and green made in 1822 with silver lace trimming and green silk ruffled sleeves. The Royal Company of Archers was founded in 1636 as the Sovereign's bodyguard in Scotland. This particular outfit was featured as one of the centrepieces of a major Tartan Exhibition, held in New York in 1988.

Above:
Pure silk velvet Doublet which was tailored from velvet woven in France.

THE SCOTTISH REGISTER OF TARTANS

On the back wall in the centre is a framed Certificate of the Scottish Register of Tartans tartan with a pattern swatch of the tartan itself beside it.

"This is the Tartan Registration Certificate of the Scottish Register of Tartans tartan which was the first tartan to be registered in the Scottish Register of Tartans on 5th February 2009. The tartan was numbered 10,000 and was designed by Kinloch Anderson.

It was in 2009 that 'The Scottish Register of Tartans' became Scotland's first official tartan register and put the recording and codification of tartans into the public domain where tartan rightfully belongs. Previously this had always been carried out by several independent private organisations. The Register is administered by the National Archives of Scotland and the Keeper of the Records of Scotland is also the Keeper of the Scottish Register of Tartans.

The Scottish Register of Tartans promotes and preserves information about registered tartans, is a focal point for tartan research and provides the tartan industry in Scotland with a platform for its expertise and quality of product.

The criteria for registration is "a design which is capable of being woven, consisting of two or more alternating coloured stripes which combine vertically and horizontally to form a repeated checked pattern". The design and the name of a new tartan must be unique to the Register and not confusingly similar to any other tartan already recorded.

Opened out in front of you is a large tartan pattern book, one of many such books in Kinloch Anderson's Collections. Every length of tartan woven for each customer was recorded and the tartan entered into one of these books for future reference.

Behind this, standing open at the back is another large tartan record book compiled by Murdo MacLeod MacDonald in the early 20th century. It was intended to be a complete record of all known tartans but it was never finished.

The Scottish Register of Tartans

This is to certify that the following tartan has met the conditions
of registration set out in
the Scottish Register of Tartans Act, 2008.

The Scottish Register of Tartans' Tartan

Registration Number: 10,000

Thread count details
K/5 M3 LT6 M3 K23 DT2 K2 DT28 T2 DT28 M2 DT2 M7 N4 M/12
Half sett, full count at pivots

Colour Details
K=BLACK; M=MAROON; LT=LIGHT TAN; DT=DARK TAN;
T=TAN; N=NEUTRAL;

Keeper of the Scottish Register of Tartans
5 February 2009

National
Records of
Scotland

The Scottish Government

Showcase 2 : CIVILIAN UNIFORMS

The Kinloch Anderson Company has made many of the official uniforms for the Royal Household and Civilian office bearers and Voluntary Brigades. The Queen's (Edinburgh) Rifle Volunteer Brigade had members who were Advocates, Writers to The Signet, Solicitors, Accountants, Bankers, Civil Servants, Merchants and High Constables.

This Case contains a Lord Lieutenants Uniform. The Lord Lieutenants and Deputy Lord Lieutenants deputise for the Sovereign in Scotland and attend official Royal functions if the Sovereign is absent. The silver trim and thistle buttons on the scarlet tunic, tailored by Kinloch Anderson in 1902, show particularly fine craftsmanship.

Behind the uniform is a painting of a Deputy Lieutenant commissioned by Kinloch Anderson so that the details of the uniform could be checked.

The centerpiece is a Queen's (Edinburgh) Rifle Volunteer Brigade Jacket.

The Brigade was formed from members of the trades and professions in Edinburgh and eventually became part of the Royal Scots (The Royal Regiment). This uniform was made in the summer of 1888 for the 2nd Lt. L.I. Cadell.

At the base of the Jacket stands a picture of Mr William Kinloch Anderson the third generation of the firm who was also a member of the Brigade and the photograph is of him dressed in his 2nd Lieutenants Uniform in 1895.

On the right hand side of the Showcase is a model wearing the current uniform of the Royal Company of Archers. Kinloch Anderson had a long association with the Royal Company of Archers, the Queen's Bodyguard in Scotland. This is an example of the modern Border Green Uniform first introduced in 1829. To be noted are features such as the wrist protector, the Bow case belt and the red Wyper – used to clean a sword if it had to be used in defence of the Crown.

Showcase 3 : MILITARY UNIFORMS

The third historic Showcase is entitled Military Uniforms. Just prior to the First World War, Military Tailoring developed into an important part of the Company's business, with Officers Uniforms being tailored for all of the famous Scottish Regiments and many others. The Company built up a reputation for the quality of its tailoring and excellent service.

There is an example of a Black Watch Officer's Full Uniform. The Black Watch Regiment was raised in 1739, under its first Colonel, John 20th Earl of Crawford. This full Dress uniform was made by Kinloch Anderson in the 1930's and features the scarlet tunic with Black Watch kilt, and belted plaid. The feather bonnet has a red feather (hackle) presented by George III to the Regiment in 1793, in recognition of gallantry shown in reclaiming British Guns from the French.

The second uniform to be featured in this Showcase is the Scots Guards Uniform. The Scots Guards were one of the oldest Regiments in the British Army, being first raised in 1642. This uniform has a scarlet tunic, navy trousers with scarlet stripe and a fine silk waist sash.

The Regimental Rams Head, made in 1910 and fitted with a snuff bowl and a holder for cigars is a magnificent feature in the centre of this Showcase. The Rams Head would have been positioned at the head of the Mess Table in front of the Colonel and would have been mounted on rollers so that it could be pushed down the table after the Loyal Toast. All the fittings on this Rams Head are sterling silver and real gemstones are used for decoration.

In front of the Rams Head are three belt buckles which were worn on the Cross Belt of the Black Watch uniform which is displayed in this Case. These Cross Belt buckles belong to the Regiments of the Royal Scots Fusiliers, the Argyll and Sutherland Highlanders and the Seaforth Highlanders.

On the back wall of the Showcase are five prints from a series of paintings by A. N. Haswell Millar which were commissioned by Kinloch Anderson in 1952. They are thought to have been produced to help check that every detail of the uniform was correct.

On the side wall of this cabinet are two William Anderson & Sons calendars for the year 1913, one of which has a picture of the new artillery Mess Kit and the other a picture of two men wearing Kinloch Anderson outfits representing Highland Dress in those times.

Above:
The Regimental Rams Head Snuff Bowl.

Showcase 4 :
HIGHLAND DRESS ACCESSORIES

This Showcase is triangular in shape to suit the corner in which it is placed and is entitled Highland Dress Accessories. The items here are rare and very valuable.

Kinloch Anderson supplied many different Highland Dress Accessories which enhanced Military and Civilian outfits.

A Sporran was the pouch or bag, used to hold everyday items. A belt pouch was common in Medieval European dress, as most clothing did not have pockets. This tradition continues in Scotland to the present day with the traditional kilt.

The Skean Dhu or Sgian Dubh is gaelic for "Black Knife". In earlier times, Highlanders concealed their Sgian Dubh beneath their clothing but it is thought that it was a courtesy not to conceal weapons when visiting homes of friends and so the knife would be placed in the stocking top. Nowadays it is worn in the kilt hose, with the hilt showing.

Other accessories on display include Belts and belt plates or buckles, kilt pins, Jabot and cuffs.

- A Skean Dhu supplied to the Queen's Own Cameron Highlanders
- A Queen's Own Cameron Highlanders Dirk includes a knife and fork and conforms to standard 1950 uniform regulations
- A Queen's Own Cameron Highlanders Officer's Sporran

- An Argyll and Sutherland Highlanders hair sporran. This is a full dress sporran with 5 Gold bullion tassels and was priced at £8.50 in the 1930s
- A Gordon Highlander's Sporran
- A pair of buckle brogue shoes to be worn with Military Dress uniform supplied by Kinloch Anderson

In the early years of the 20th century the Kinloch Anderson Company was already looking to overseas markets and producing clothing and accessories to be sold abroad. Reservist Military Regiments comprising of volunteers of Scottish descent were formed in countries such as Canada and South Africa. Many of these regiments based their uniforms on traditional Highland Dress and Kinloch Anderson supplied these regiments with their Dress Uniform. On display are a collection of Sporrans that were produced and sold to volunteer and overseas Regiments.

- 48 Highlanders of Canada
- Transvaal Scottish Volunteer Regiment (South Africa)
- Liverpool Scottish – a Regiment formed from Scottish Volunteers living in Liverpool in 1900
- A collection of Company catalogues and calendars that were sent around the world to Scottish Officers serving overseas and to overseas Regiments

Kinloch Anderson's booklet *The Scottish National Dress* is opened to show the range of accessories supplied by Kinloch Anderson and the prices of these items in those days.

Above:
A Queen's Own Cameron Highlanders Dirk includes a knife and fork and conforms to standard 1950 uniform regulations.

Panel 1 :
THE HERITAGE OF KINLOCH ANDERSON

There follows a series of Panels taking you through the heritage of Kinloch Anderson's Clothing Manufacturing, Ladies Skirts and Kiltmaking.

The Heritage of Kinloch Anderson panel features a picture of the original George Street Shop in 1890, a Kinloch Anderson Shop interior of 1940 and the outside double façade of the Kinloch Anderson Shop in George Street in 1960. It also features John Knox's House in the High Street, Edinburgh which is one of Edinburgh's oldest surviving buildings from where Kinloch Anderson sold Scottish clothing and accessories, mostly to tourists.

The panel writing reads: "From 1868 the Kinloch Anderson Company had its base in Edinburgh's famous George Street. The original shop was sited at no. 15, before moving to no. 17 and eventually becoming based at 14–16 George Street for nearly a century. During this time, Kinloch Anderson became renowned throughout Scotland and beyond, as Scotland's premier civilian tailors. Before the First World War the company expanded into making Military Uniforms. In the 1930's William Kinloch Anderson introduced ready to wear men's clothing. By the 1950's WJ Kinloch Anderson, the fourth generation, travelled frequently to Canada and USA and in order to meet the increasing demand in the post war period, particularly in North America, and a Wholesale Division was established to supply clothing and accessories in tartans and tweeds. In the 1970's Douglas Kinloch Anderson, the fifth generation, expanded sales into the ladies clothing business in Japan and in 1979 the company was awarded The Queens Award for Export Achievement. The story of the further expansion in the Far East and development of the Company continues round this exhibition."

Also shown on this Panel is a picture of Kinloch Anderson long service employees in 1925 and a picture of Kinloch Anderson staff in 1890. It features a copy of the annual sales of the Company for its first 25 years of existence from 1869 to 1894 which shows a steady increase from £1,561 to £9,260 per annum!

The Rules and Instructions to staff in 1925 are also there to be read. Staff were left in no doubt what was expected of them and each one received a booklet of 12 pages of Rules and Instructions finishing with a page of 10 things to remember which included:

- *Be economical in large and small matters: save paper, string, lights etc.*
- *Win your customer's confidence and only sell them goods which are entirely suitable for their particular requirements.*
- *If all assistants give due consideration and attention to every rule the day's work will be easier for all concerned.*

Above:
Kinloch Anderson Longservice Award
Ceremony 1925

The Heritage of Kinloch Anderson

From 1868 the Kinloch Anderson Company had its base in Edinburgh's famous George Street. The original shop was sited at no 15, before moving to no 17 and eventually becoming based at 14 -16 George Street for nearly a century. During this time, Kinloch Anderson became renowned throughout Scotland and beyond, as Scotland's premier civilian tailors. Before the First World War the company expanded into making Military Uniforms. In the 1930's William Kinloch Anderson introduced ready to wear men's clothing. By the 1950's WJ Kinloch Anderson, the fourth generation, travelled frequently to Canada and USA and in order to meet the increasing demand in the post war period, particularly in North America, and a Wholesale Division was established to supply clothing and accessories in tartans and tweeds. In the 1970's Douglas Kinloch Anderson, the fifth generation, expanded sales into the ladies clothing business in Japan and in 1979 the company was awarded The Queens Award for Export Achievement. The story of the further expansion in the Far East and development of the Company continues round this exhibition.

Kinloch Anderson shop 1940's

George Street Shop 1890

Kinloch Anderson shop interior 1940

Kinloch Anderson Longservice Award Ceremony 1925

Kinloch Anderson Staff 1890

Accounts
Copy of the Annual Sales of the Company for its first 25 years of existence from 1869 - 1894, a steady increase from £1561 - £9260 per annum!

Rules and Written Rules

In 1926 staff were left in no doubt what was expected of them and each one received a booklet of twelve pages of Rules and Instructions - finishing with a page of 10 things to remember which included:

- Be economical in large and small matters: save paper, string, lights etc.
- Win your customer's confidence and only sell them goods which are entirely suitable for their particular requirements.
- If all assistants give due consideration and attention to every rule the day's work will be easier for all concerned.

John Knox's House
Kinloch Anderson at John Knox House, High Street, Edinburgh, one of Edinburgh's oldest surviving buildings

Panel 2: CLOTHING MANUFACTURING

Important technical innovations, created by the company itself were a vital part of translating traditional skills into modern production methods.

In 1980 the Digital Electronic Chalking System (DECS) – a unique specialist computer controlled machine - was devised by Kinloch Anderson. In one day the DECS machine could chalk and check match to the highest degree of accuracy as many garments as a hand chalker used to chalk in two weeks.

A picture of the Kinloch Anderson Restalrig Factory where these skirts were made also shows the large Kinloch Anderson delivery van - quite unlike the modern delivery vans of today.

Furthermore for over 15 years the Company had a skirt production factory unit in Ayrshire and there is a picture of this factory in 1981. The Kinloch Anderson Company move to Leith was made in 1990.

Panel 3: LADIES SKIRTS

The panel on Ladies' Skirts explains that in the 1970s and 1980s ladies 'classic fashion' was very popular and Kinloch Anderson made over 100,000 pure wool tartan and plain coloured skirts a year. In 1979 the Company received The Queen's Award for Export.

Markets were predominantly in Europe, North America and Japan, and Kinloch Anderson skirts were sold in many prestigious stores in these countries.

Beside a picture of Scotland House in Alexandria, Virginia, USA is written: "Other Scottish clothing and accessories were also exported at that time, mostly for Scots living in North America or to the American tourist market in Bermuda. For many years Kinloch Anderson owned and ran its own shop "Scotland House" in Alexandria, Virginia."

Finally there is a picture of a Kinloch Anderson Concession Shop at Harrods. The Company also manufactured skirt ranges for famous brands including *Burberry, Prada, Daks, Aquascutum, Pringle, The Scotch House, Ballantyne* and *Lyle and Scott* and many more.

Clothing Manufacturing

HRH The Princess Royal inspects the DECS machine at the Restalrig factory July 1988

Important technical innovations, created by the company itself were a vital part of translating traditional skills into modern production methods.

In 1980 the Digital Electronic Chalking Systems (DECS) - a unique specialist computer controlled machine - was devised by Kinloch Anderson. In one day the DECS machine could chalk and check match to the highest degree of accuracy as many garments as a hand chalker used to do in two weeks.

Restalrig Factory
At the same time Kinloch Anderson had a large factory and warehouse at Restalrig, Edinburgh.

Muirkirk Factory Ayrshire
For over 15 years the Company had a skirt production factory unit in Ayrshire.

This is the Kinloch Anderson factory in 1981

The move to this current site in Leith was made in 1990

Ladies Skirts

In the 1970's and 1980's ladies "classic fashion" was very popular and Kinloch Anderson made over 100,000 pure wool tartan and plain coloured skirts a year. In 1979 the Company received The Queen's Award for Export. Markets were predominantly in Europe, North America and Japan, and Kinloch Anderson skirts were sold in many prestigious stores in these countries.

In 1998 Kinloch Anderson won the Edinburgh and Lothians Business Excellence Award for Manufacturing and Distribution.

Scotland House

Scotland House
Other Scottish clothing and accessories were also exported at that time, mostly for Scots living in North America or to the American tourist market in Bermuda. For many years Kinloch Anderson owned and ran its own shop "Scotland House in Alexandria, Virginia.

Famous Brands
The company has also manufactured skirt ranges for famous brands including Burberry, Prada, Daks, Aquascutum, Pringle, Harrods, The Scotch House, Ballantyne and Lyle and Scott.

Kinloch Anderson at Harrods

Panel 4 : KILTMAKING

The Kiltmaking panel explains and illustrates how Kinloch Anderson have been market leaders in the evolution of kiltmaking and Highland Dress since 1868.

Creating a traditional man's kilt requires knowledge, expertise and painstaking craftsmanship. Traditionally all that is required is a needle and thread, chalk, a tape measure and a lifetime of skill and experience!

The pictures illustrate the amount of cloth which goes into making a full man's kilt, hand-chalking, hand-stitching, measuring each pleat, cutting away the fabric inside the kilt, pressing-in pleats, putting in stay tape, covering the button hole, sewing on the canvas, attaching buckles, pattern matching belt loops, sewing-in the lining, the final press and quality control.

An example of a kilt pleated to sett, a kilt pleated to line and a box pleated are also pictured.

VIEWING WINDOW

You now come to a Viewing Window where you can look through into the Kinloch Anderson Production Unit and see the action actually taking place whether it be hand sewing, chalking, tear and match, pattern cutting, pressing or passing. There is an illustrated chart to show you where each of these activities is taking place.

Above the window is a brass copy of the full page feature in *The Scotsman* newspaper headed Kinloch Anderson £1 million for Export.

Right:
The Viewing Window onto the
Kinloch Anderson Production Unit

Kilt Making

Kinloch Anderson has been market leader in the evolution of kiltmaking and Highland Dress since 1868.
Creating a traditional Man's kilt requires knowledge, expertise and painstaking craftmanship. Traditionally all that is required is a needle and thread, chalk, a tape measure and a lifetime of skill and experience!

This is the amount of cloth which goes into making a full man's kilt (over 8 yards!)

Traditional Kilt Maker

Hand chalk pleats

An important skill is chalking out the best pleat setting for each individual tartan design.

Hand stitch in pleats

Measure each pleat for perfect fit

There are between 23 and 43 pleats in a Kinloch Anderson kilt, depending on the sett of the tartan.

Cut away fabric inside the kilt

After initial pleating the excess cloth at the back is cut away so that the kilt is not too bulky around the waist.

First Press putting in pleats

Put in stay tape and covering button hole

Sew on canvas

Tape is attached round the strap holes to avoid wear and tear.
Canvas lining gives strength to the back of the kilt for cover, strength and fit.

Attach buckles

Pattern match belt loops

Sew in Lining

Sewing on some of the finishing touches - soft leather straps and silver buckles

Final Press

Quality Control

The kilts are then checked and pressed to ensure they meet our exacting standards

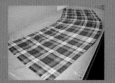

Pleated to set

Pleated to Line

Box Pleated

The kilt can be pleated in a number of ways to achieve a different effect

OFFICERS UNIFORMS
FOR SCOTTISH REGIMENTS

In the early part of the 20th century, Kinloch Anderson supplied Officers Uniforms for all the famous Scottish Regiments.

To the right of the window a large wall features meticulously painted pictures showing full details of the Officers' Uniforms which were supplied by Kinloch Anderson. There were 10 Regiments at that time and beside each picture is a mounted swatch of the tartan associated with that particular Regiment. These were as follows:

*   The Hunting Stewart tartan worn by
    the Royal Scots
*   The Government tartan worn by
    the Royal Scots Fusiliers
*   The Leslie tartan worn by
    the King's Own Scottish Borderers

*   The Douglas tartan worn by the Cameronians
*   The Government tartan (Black Watch sett) worn
    by the Black Watch (Royal Highlanders)
*   The MacKenzie tartan (Highland Light Infantry
    sett) worn by the Highland Light Infantry
*   The MazKenzie tartan (Seaforth sett) worn by
    the Seaforth Highlanders
*   The Gordon tartan worn by
    the Gordon Highlanders
*   The Cameron of Erracht tartan worn by
    the Queen's Own Cameron Highlanders
*   The Government tartan (Sutherland sett) worn
    by the Argyll and Sutherland Highlanders

On 28th March 2006 the last four remaining Regiments were amalgamated into the Royal Regiment of Scotland and the Government 1A (Black Watch) tartan was adopted as its regimental tartan.

In the early part of the 20th Century Kinloch Anderson supplied Officers' Uniforms for all the famous Scottish Regiments.

On the 28th March 2006 the last four remaining Regiments were amalgamated into the Royal Regiment of Scotland and the Government 1A (Black Watch) tartan was adopted as its Regimental tartan.

Above:
Meticulously painted pictures showing full details of the Officers' Uniforms together with their respective tartans.

20TH CENTURY HIGHLAND DRESS

The next adjacent wall features 20th Century Highland Dress. The Duke of Windsor requested some special Highland Dress designs from Kinloch Anderson who commissioned these sketches from the artist A.N. Haswell Millar.

Beneath these Haswell Millar prints are four fine coloured illustrations of Kinloch Anderson Highland Dress in the 20th century. These feature in The Scottish National Dress, a handbook produced by Wm Anderson & Sons for everyone interested in Highland Dress, of which five editions were printed.

DIGITAL SCREEN

Your walk round the Heritage Room now brings you to the large Digital Screen which allows you to choose how you would like to learn more about Kinloch Anderson. You can click the mouse on "Six Generations", "Historical Catalogues", "Kinloch Anderson Today", "Kilts and Highland Dress", "The Complete Tartan Design Service available from Kinloch Anderson", "Making Kilts", "Videos" or "Womenswear". Perhaps the most popular is the Kinloch Anderson video which brings the story of Kinloch Anderson, Scotland to life in a few minutes of time.

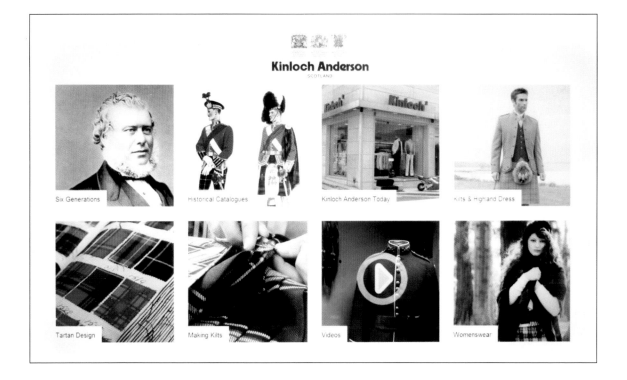

Below:
This photograph of His Majesty King
George VI came from Buckingham Palace
in 1952 after the King had died. It was sent
by The Queen Mother along with the letter,
to Mr W J Kinloch Anderson, the fourth
generation of the Company.

By Appointment to
Her Majesty The Queen
Tailors and Kiltmakers
Kinloch Anderson Ltd

By Appointment to
HRH The Duke of Edinburgh
Tailors and Kiltmakers
Kinloch Anderson Ltd

By Appointment to
HRH The Prince of Wales
Tailors and Kiltmakers
Kinloch Anderson Ltd

Kinloch Anderson
SCOTLAND

Panel 5 :
ROYAL WARRANTS

Beside the screen and high on the wall you see a special wooden plaque on which are mounted Kinloch Anderson's three Royal Warrants. The next panel beneath is entitled The Royal Warrants.

Over the years, Kinloch Anderson has received many accolades, but particular pride is taken in The Royal Warrants of Appointment as Tailors and Kiltmakers to HM The Queen, HRH The Duke of Edinburgh and HRH The Prince of Wales.

BUCKINGHAM PALACE

November 3rd, 1952

Dear Mr. Anderson,

I am now commanded by
Queen Elizabeth the Queen Mother
to send you the enclosed photograph
of The King, which Her Majesty thinks
you will like to have in memory of
the past few years, when you served
His Majesty.

Yours sincerely,

Katharine Seymour
Lady-in-Waiting.

W.J. Kinloch Anderson, Esq.

The concept of the Royal Warrant of Appointment dates back to the advent of the monarchy. By the 15th century, Royal Tradesmen were appointed formally in writing by means of a Royal Warrant issued by the Lord Chamberlain, a practice which continues to this day.

The Royal Warrant has always been a recognition of personal service of the highest order. It is granted to a named individual within the company who is then responsible for ensuring that the Warrant is correctly used.

In order to be considered for the granting of a Royal Warrant of Appointment, a company must supply the member of the Royal Family concerned, or their Household, with products or services in significant quantity over a period of time.

The final decision to grant a Royal Warrant of Appointment is made by the member of the Royal Family concerned and if a Royal Warrant is appointed, the Company must thereafter abide by the strict rules which govern the use and display of Royal Arms associated with the name of the Grantor.

Kinloch Anderson first supplied HM King Edward VII in 1903 but the first Royal Warrant was granted by HM King George V in 1934 and another thereafter by HM King George VI. Today, Kinloch Anderson holds Royal Warrants of Appointment as Tailors and Kiltmakers to Her Majesty The Queen since 1955, His Royal Highness The Duke of Edinburgh since 1960 and His Royal Highness The Price of Wales since 1980.

The panel features a letter from Buckingham Palace in 1903 which confirms that the Company has served members of The Royal Family for many years. There is a photograph of His Majesty King George VI which, when he died in 1952, was sent by the Queen Mother to Mr W J Kinloch Anderson, the fourth generation of the Company's family.

There is a photograph of the Royal Wedding of Princess Elizabeth to Prince Philip, the Duke of Edinburgh on 20th November 1947 and of the page boys Princes William and Michael wearing Royal Stewart kilts made by Kinloch Anderson, personally signed and sent with a letter from St James's Palace to W J Kinloch Anderson. There is

Royal Warrants

Over the years, Kinloch Anderson has received many accolades, but particular pride is taken in The Royal Warrants of Appointment as Tailors and Kiltmakers to HM The Queen, HRH The Duke of Edinburgh and HRH The Prince of Wales.

In order to be considered for the granting of a Royal Warrant of Appointment, a company must supply the member of the Royal Family concerned, or their household, with a significant quantity of products or services over a considerable period of time.

The Royal Warrant has always been recognition of personal service of the highest order. It is granted to a named individual within the company who is then responsible for ensuring that the Warrant is correctly used. The final decision to grant a Royal Warrant of Appointment is made by the member of the Royal Family concerned and there are strict rules which govern the use and display of the Warrants.

As shown by the letter from Buckingham Palace in 1903, the Company has served members of The Royal Family for many years. The first Royal Warrant of Appointment was granted by George VI in 1934.

Pageboys Princes William and Michael wear Royal Stewart kilts made by Kinloch Anderson. A photograph of the Pageboys was sent from St. James' Palace to W.T Kinloch Anderson, signed by both Princes.

Royal Wedding Pageboys

Royal Wedding

This photograh of His Majesty King George VI was sent when he died in 1952 by The Queen Mother to Mr WJ Kinloch Anderson, the fourth generation in the Company family.

The Duke of York was supplied by the Company even before he became King George VI as can be seen from the letter written in his own hand, from Glamis Castle, the family home of Her Majesty The Queen Mother.

The Royal Wedding of Princess Elizabeth to Prince Philip, Duke of Edinburgh, 20th November 1947.

Prince Charles and The Duchess of Cornwall wearing a Lord of the Isles long silk skirt.

The Queen and The Duke of Edinburgh with Princes Andrew and Edward at the Braemar Highland Gathering

The Queen with Prince Philip

Prince Edward, Duke of Wessex with Sophie, Duchess of Wessex

The Royal Family at Balmoral April 1999
Pictured from left to right:
HRH The Duke of York, Earl of Inverness
The Prince of Wales, Duke of Rothesay,
Prince Harry, Prince Edward, Earl of Wessex,
The Princess Royal, Prince William,
Miss Zara Philips, Princesses Beatrice and Euginie
and The Duke of Edinburgh

HRH The Prince of Wales with Camilla the Duchess of Cornwall leaving Crathie Church near Balmoral on their first Wedding Anniversary Sunday 9th April 2006.

HR The Prince of Wales with Princes William and Harry

Right:
The Royal Wedding of
Princess Elizabeth and
Prince Philip, Duke of
Edinburgh, on
20th November 1947.

Below:
Photograph of Prince
William and Prince
Michael sent with a letter
from the Duchess of
Gloucester, York House,
St James's Palace to
Mr W J Kinloch Anderson
on 12th June 1948.

YORK HOUSE,
ST. JAMES'S PALACE.

June 12th 1948

Dear Mr Anderson,

The Duchess of Gloucester
desires me to send you this photograph of
Prince William and Prince Michael which she
thought you might care to have, and which
you will notice they have both signed. This
was taken at the time of Princess Elizabeth's
wedding last November.

Yours sincerely,

Lady-in-Waiting.

W.T. Kinloch Anderson Esq., J.P.,

William. Michael

a photograph of Prince Charles in a Royal Stewart
kilt outfit with the Duchess of Cornwall wearing a
Lord of the Isles long kilted skirt. There is a
photograph of HRH The Prince of Wales with the
Duchess of Cornwall leaving Crathie Church near
Balmoral on their first wedding anniversary,
Sunday 9th April 2006.

The Queen and Duke of Edinburgh are shown with
Princes Andrew and Edward at the Braemar
Highland Gathering. Prince Edward, Duke of
Wessex is shown wearing his Balmoral tartan day

kilt outfit alongside his wife, the Duchess of Wessex. A picture of the Royal Family at Balmoral April 1999 features HRH Duke of York, The Earl of Inverness; The Prince of Wales; The Duke of Rothesay; Prince Harry; Prince Edward, The Earl of Wessex; The Princess Royal; Prince William; Miss Zara Phillips; Princess Beatrice; Princess Eugenie; The Duke the Edinburgh and Her Majesty The Queen.

Another photograph shows the Queen wearing an Old Stewart tartan kilt and the Duke of Edinburgh wearing a Balmoral tartan kilt and finally the Prince of Wales is shown in the grounds of Balmoral Castle together with Princes William and Harry.

Top Left:
HRH The Prince of Wales and the Duchess of Cornwall on their first wedding anniversary, 9th April 2006.

Below Right:
HRH Prince Edward, Earl of Wessex with the Countess of Wessex, Edinburgh, August 2003.

Bottom Left:
HRH The Prince of Wales at Balmoral with Princes William and Harry.

Panel 6 :
ROYAL FAMILY TARTAN CONNECTIONS

The next panel features The Royal Family Tartan Connections. Due to their Stewart (Stuart) ancestry, the Royal Family wear the Stewart Tartans. The name of Stewart used by the Royal House was spelled Stuart after Mary Queen of Scots' time in France. The Royal Stewarts had their residences at Holyrood Palace, Edinburgh, at Linlithgow, birthplace of Mary Queen of Scots and Falkland Palace in Fife.

Charles Edward Stuart (Bonnie Prince Charlie) is perhaps the best known of the Stuarts for the uprising he led that was crushed at Culloden Moor in 1746. He aimed to replace the Hanoverians with the Stuart Dynasty.

It was not until a century later that Queen Victoria, who was proud of her own Stuart descent, completed the rehabilitation of the Stuart name.

Each tartan is displayed beside a photograph of a member of The Royal Family wearing it.

Above:
HRH The Prince of Wales wearing a Dress Stewart tartan kilt on a Royal Visit to Edinburgh July 1979.

Top Centre:
HRH The Duke of Edinburgh wearing a Royal Stewart tartan kilt at the Royal Scottish Pipers Society Centenary Ball at the Assembly Rooms, Edinburgh, June 1982.

The Royal Stewart tartan is one of the most universally known tartans.

The Dress Stewart tartan was created primarily for dress or evening wear

Royal Family Tartan Connections

The Stewart Tartans

Due to their Stewart (Stuart) ancestry, the Royal Family wear the Stewart Tartans. The name of Stewart used by the Royal House was spelled Stuart after Mary Queen of Scots' time in France. The Royal Stewarts had their residences at Holyrood Palace, Edinburgh, at Linlithgow, birthplace of Mary Queen of Scots and Falkland in Fife. Charles Edward Stuart (Bonnie Prince Charlie) is perhaps best known of the Stuarts for the uprising he led that was crushed at Culloden Moor in 1745.

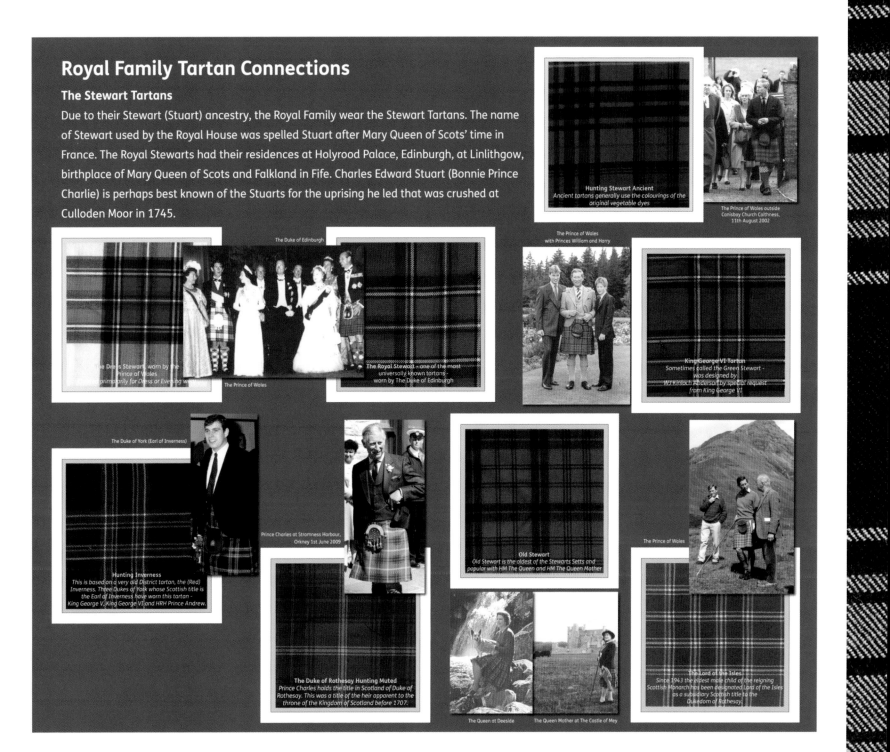

Hunting Stewart Ancient
Ancient tartans generally use the colourings of the original vegetable dyes

The Prince of Wales outside Canisbay Church Caithness, 11th August 2002

The Duke of Edinburgh

The Prince of Wales

The Dress Stewart, worn by the Prince of Wales
Used primarily for Dress or Evening wear

The Royal Stewart - one of the most universally known tartans - worn by The Duke of Edinburgh

The Prince of Wales with Princes William and Harry

King George VI Tartan
Sometimes called the Green Stewart - was designed by WJ Kinloch Anderson by special request from King George VI.

The Duke of York (Earl of Inverness)

Prince Charles at Stromness Harbour, Orkney 1st June 2009

Hunting Inverness
This is based on a very old District tartan, the (Red) Inverness. Three Dukes of York whose Scottish title is the Earl of Inverness have worn this tartan - King George V, King George VI and HRH Prince Andrew.

Old Stewart
Old Stewart is the oldest of the Stewarts Setts and popular with HM The Queen and HM The Queen Mother

The Prince of Wales

The Duke of Rothesay Hunting Muted
Prince Charles holds the title in Scotland of Duke of Rothesay. This was a title of the heir apparent to the throne of the Kingdom of Scotland before 1707.

The Queen at Deeside

The Queen Mother at The Castle of Mey

The Lord of the Isles
Since 1943 the eldest male child of the reigning Scottish Monarch has been designated Lord of the Isles as a subsidiary Scottish title to the Dukedom of Rothesay.

The Old Stewart tartan
was popular with HM The Queen and HM The
Queen Mother. It is one of the oldest Stewart
tartan setts.

The Hunting Stewart Ancient tartan.
Ancient tartans generally use the colourways of the
original vegetable dyes.

Above:
HM The Queen wearing the Old Stewart
tartan at Deeside.

Top Right:
HRH The Prince of Wales wearing a
Hunting Stewart Ancient tartan kilt,
Caithness, 11th August 2002.

Bottom Right:
HRH Prince of Wales wearing a King
George VI (Green Stewart) tartan kilt with
his sons Princes William and Harry.

King George VI tartan
– sometimes called the Green Stewart tartan –
was designed by W J Kinloch Anderson by
special request from King George VI.

The Hunting Inverness Tartan is based on a very old District tartan, the (Red) Inverness. The Dukes of York have traditionally also held the title of The Earl of Inverness, and have worn this tartan. They include King George V, King George VI and HRH Prince Andrew, The Earl of Inverness.

The Lord of the Isles tartan. Since 1493 the eldest male child of the reigning Scottish Monarch has been designated Lord of the Isles as an alternative Scottish title to The Duke of Rothesay.

The Duke of Rothesay Hunting Muted tartan. The Duke of Rothesay has been the title of the heir apparent to the throne of the Kingdom of Scotland for many centuries and the title is held by Prince Charles.

Since the refurbishment of the Heritage Room a new tartan connection has emerged. The latest Royal Family tartan association comes with the Scottish titles of the Duke and Duchess of Cambridge as the Earl and Countess of Strathearn.

Top Left:
HRH Prince Andrew wearing a kilt in the Hunting Inverness tartan.

Top Right:
The Duchess of Rothesay wearing a long silk skirt in the Lord of the Isles tartan at Holyrood Palace, 4th June 2008.

Bottom Left:
HRH The Prince of Wales wearing a kilt in the Duke of Rothesay Hunting Muted tartan at Stromness Harbour, Orkney on 1st June 2009.

Bottom Right:
The Countess of Strathearn wearing a specially woven silk scarf in the Strathearn tartan at Dumfries House, Ayrshire on 29th March 2013.

There is now a corner Showcase entitled
The Balmoral Tartan and Sovereign's Piper.

The Balmoral Tartan was designed in 1857 by
HRH Prince Albert, Prince
Consort for Her Majesty
Queen Victoria, and was
named after their castle and
estate in Deeside. The tartan is
the Private property of
reigning monarch and other
members of the Royal Family
may wear it only in
accordance with the wishes
of the Sovereign.

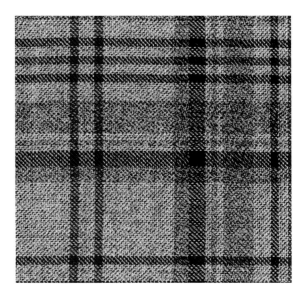

Above: The Balmoral tartan includes unusual twisted yarns
composed of different ratios of black and white threads
reflecting the granite stone which is typical of the Deeside
area including Balmoral Castle itself.

Apart from The Royal Family,
The Sovereign's Piper is
uniquely authorised to wear
the Balmoral Tartan.
The position of personal
piper to the Sovereign was
instituted by Queen Victoria
and until 1965 was a civilian
appointment. It is now
awarded to an experienced
serving Pipe Major on
secondment from the army.

The duties of the Sovereign's
Piper require that he moves
with the court and plays daily
at nine o'clock in the morning
wherever the Sovereign is in
residence. At Balmoral Castle,

Holyrood Palace and at Windsor Castle he
frequently plays at dinner.

The centrepiece of this Showcase is the Sovereign's
Piper's Patrol Jacket. This jacket has 8 Royal
Crown gold buttons, a pocket badge with a large
EIIR and Crown embroidered in gold thread, 2
EIIR gold badges on the collar, epaulettes with gold
braid, 4 gold braid rank stripes and a Pipe Major's
gold embroidered laurel wreath arm badge.

A picture of Pipe Major Alastair Cuthbertson, the
Sovereign's Piper from 2006 to 2008, is seen here
wearing this Patrol Jacket at Buckingham Palace.

Right:
HM The Queen and HRH The
Duke of Edinburgh. Balmoral 1998.

Far Right:
Young Prince Charles at Balmoral.

The large central background picture in this cabinet shows Her Majesty The Queen with His Royal Highness The Duke of Edinburgh wearing his kilt in the Balmoral tartan with a grey tweed jacket and waistcoat.

Also in this cabinet are four different fabric samples of the Balmoral tartan in different weights of cloth and the sett woven in different sizes. Each is accompanied by a Royal photograph wearing the particular fabric on display. There is a picture of Prince Charles as a small boy, probably aged about 5, wearing his kilt and jacket, a photograph in black and white of King Edward VIII at Ballater Station in Deeside wearing a blanket weight Balmoral tartan kilt with a length of the tartan thrown over his shoulder like a plaid, a picture of the Princess Royal with young Peter Phillips in a kilt and little Zara Phillips in a Balmoral tartan kilted skirt and a picture of the Prince of Wales wearing his Balmoral tartan kilt with the Duchess of Cornwall wearing her Balmoral tartan skirt and tartan trimmed jacket.

Another photograph features Pipe Major Brian McRae, the Sovereign's Piper from 1980 - 1995 wearing the full and Evening Dress as worn when in Scotland. The kilt and plaid are in the Balmoral tartan, the pipe ribbons are Royal Stewart and Dress Stewart. The fine silver badges and appointments display the Royal Crest of Scotland and the pipe banner carries the Royal Arms in gold embroidery on a blue silk ground.

Panel 7 :
TARTAN DESIGN AND DEVELOPMENT

To the right of this Showcase is the Tartan Design and Development panel providing information about the design and development of exclusive tartans.

It is a specialist activity of Kinloch Anderson to respond to the needs of companies or individuals who value and wish to enhance their identity and their image with their own exclusively designed tartan.

Great importance is placed on the historical background of the organization or the family and the association with Scotland.

The customers design and colour ideas are discussed and carefully researched.

The initial design ideas are worked out using computer printouts giving a variety of options to consider.

Services include yarn colour expertise, fabric advice and sett size recommendations.

Experience and knowledge is given as to how a flat tartan picture will transpose into woven cloth.

Kinloch Anderson can develop a new tartan from concept right through to the manufacture and supply of exclusive clothing, gifts and accessories.

The accompanying illustrations in this regard are: Barbour, Drambuie, the Edinburgh Zoo Panda, Commonwealth Games Team Scotland, British Caledonian Airways the first corporate project in 1985, and also 5 family tartans.

Tartan Design and Development

Design and development of exclusive tartans

A specialist activity of Kinloch Anderson is to respond to the needs of companies, institutions, societies or families who value and wish to enhance their identity and their image with their own exclusively designed tartan.

Great importance is placed on the historical background of the organisations or the family and their association with Scotland.

The customers design and colour ideas are discussed and carefully researched

The initial design ideas are worked out using computer printouts giving a variety of options to consider

Services include yarn colour expertise, fabric advice and sett size recommendations

Experience and knowledge is given as to how a flat tartan picture will transpose into woven cloth

Kinloch Anderson can develop a new tartan from concept right through to manufacture and the supply of exclusive clothing, gifts and accessories.

These are some of our customers for whom an exclusive tartan has been designed and developed

Barbour

Drambuie

The Edinburgh Zoo Panda Tartan

The Scottish Commonwealth Games
Teams of 2006 and 2010

British Caledonian Airways

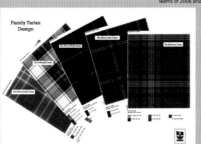

Family Tartan's

TARTAN IDENTITY

Over the years Kinloch Anderson are proud to have worked with some iconic brands. Tartans have been designed for a wide range of companies, societies, institutions and also for commemorative occasions. The Tartan Identity panel in the Heritage Room Museum is a feature. The panel is a large and curved. There are named tartan fabric samples of 36 tartan identity Kinloch Anderson customers, each identified with the year in which the tartan was designed.

Caledonian Airways 1985
Glenlivet 1987
National Galleries of Scotland 1991
Royal Warrant Holders Association 1994
St Andrews Old Course 1994
McEwans 1856, 1995
The City of Edinburgh 1997
American Express 1997
Irn Bru 1997
The Law Society of Scotland 1997
Scottish Power 1997
Barbour 1998
Drambuie 1998
The Royal College of Surgeons of Edinburgh 1998
The Scotsman Newspaper 1999
Dewars Highlander 2000
Intelligent Finance 2000
Chivas Regal 2001
Royal College of General Practitioners 2001
Chartered Institute of Bankers in Scotland 2002
Edinburgh International Conference Centre 2002
St Andrews University 2002
Glenmorangie 2003
St George's School 2003
Royal Yacht Britannia 2005
Commonwealth Games Team Scotland 2006
Erskine Veterans 2006
Institute of Directors 2007
Queen Margaret University 2007
Basel Tattoo 2008
Royal Bahrain 2008
Edinburgh Napier University 2009
Scottish Register of Tartans 2009
Scottish Tourist Guide Association 2009
Bruntsfield Links Golfing Society 2011
Edinburgh Zoo Panda 2011

Tartan is a gift that Scotland has given to the world

Tartan Identity

Over the years, Kinloch Anderson are proud to have worked with some iconic brands.
Tartans have been designed for a wide range of companies, societies, institutions and also for commemorative occasions

Caledonian Airways 1985

Glenlivet 1987

National Galleries of Scotland 1991

Royal Warrant Holders Association 1994

St Andrews Old Course 1994

McEwans 1856 1995

The City of Edinburgh 1997

American Express 1997

Irn Bru 1997

Law Society of Scotland 1997

Scottish Power 1997

Barbour 1998

Drambuie 1998

Royal College of Surgeons of Edinburgh 1998

The Scotsman Newspaper 1999

Dewars Highlander 2000

Intelligent Finance 2000

Chivas Regal 2001

Royal College of General Practitioners 2001

Chartered Institute of Bankers in Scotland 2002

Edinburgh International Conference Centre 2002

St Andrews University 2002

Glenmorangie 2003

St George's School 2003

Royal Yacht Britannia 2005

Commonwealth Games Team Scotland 2006

Erskine Veterans 2006

Institute of Directors 2007

Queen Margaret University 2007

Basel Tattoo 2008

Royal Bahrain 2008

Edinburgh Napier University 2009

Scottish Register of Tartans 2009

Scottish Tourist Guides Association 1999

Bruntsfield Links Golfing Society 2011

Edinburgh Zoo Panda 2011

Panel 9 : BRAND DEVELOPMENT

The last panel is entitled Brand Development. This has become the most entrepreneurial and global Division of the Company.

The *Kinloch Anderson Brand* name stands for "The best of British styling and fashion with a Scottish emphasis", sometimes shortened to "British Style – Scottish Character". This brand identity reflects the heritage of Kinloch Anderson and the lifestyle of Scotland.

Starting in Japan in the 1980s, Kinloch Anderson developed licensee partnerships with top quality manufacturers, who produced and marketed in their respective countries, menswear, ladieswear, childrenswear, leathergoods, shoes, household textiles and accessories such as umbrellas, gift items and watches.

In the 1990s these developments expanded into Taiwan and South Korea, and a major project of expansion in China commenced in 2012. There are now more than 300 Kinloch Anderson Shops in Asia.

Another development in the Korean market in the 2000s was the opening of shops under the *Kinloch by Kinloch Anderson* and *Kinloch 2* brand names. These ranges of menswear were designed for a younger fashionable consumer, but still reflect Kinloch Anderson's high quality standards.

An additional support for the brand in Asia has been the launching of the Kinloch Anderson range of Scotch Whiskies.

The Kinloch Anderson shops featured on this panel are:

Menswear Korea, *Kinloch2* Menswear Korea, *Kinloch by Kinloch Anderson* Menswear Korea, Childrenswear Taiwan and Ladieswear Taiwan.

DIGITAL SCREEN

Finally, there is a digital screen beside the Brand Development panel which slowly moves through some of the product ranges which have been developed under licence in the Far East under the *Kinloch Anderson Brand* name. This Division of the Company has developed and expanded rapidly and therefore the digital screen allows us to keep our customers and our visitors up to date with all the new shops and product ranges as they are established in markets overseas.

Brand Development

The Kinloch Anderson brand name stands for "The best of British styling and fashion with a Scottish emphasis", sometimes shortened to "British Style - Scottish Character". This brand identity reflects the heritage of Kinloch Anderson and the lifestyle of Scotland.

Starting in Japan in the 1980s, Kinloch Anderson have developed licensee partnerships with top quality manufacturers, who produce and market in their respective countries, menswear, ladieswear, childrenswear, leather goods, shoes, household textiles and accessories such as umberellas, gift items and watches.

In the 1990s these developments expanded into Taiwan and South Korea, and a major project of expansion in China commenced in 2012. There are now more than 300 Kinloch Anderson shops in Asia developed in co-operation with the Company's Design Team here in Scotland.

Another expansion in the Korean market in the 2000s was the opening of shops under the "Kinloch by Kinloch Anderson" and "Kinloch 2" brand names. These ranges of menswear are designed for a younger fashionable consumer, but still reflect Kinloch Anderson's high quality standards.

An additional support for the brand in Asia has been the launching of the Kinloch Anderson range of Scotch Whiskies.

Menswear, Korea

Kinloch 2 Menswear, Korea

Kinloch by Kinloch Anderson Menswear, Korea

Childrenswear, Taiwan

Ladieswear, Taiwan

" We hope that you enjoyed your 'walk' round the Kinloch Anderson Heritage Room and we look forward to welcoming you in person in the not too distant future. "

ACKNOWLEDGEMENTS

The Kinloch Anderson Retail Shop

Sir Eric Kinloch Anderson – for the Foreword and editorial contributions and assistance with historic information on Sir Walter Scott and King George IV in The Historic Journey Of Highland Dress chapter (page 15).

Constable Mark Muir – for assistance with the chapter The Historic Journey of Highland Dress (pages 18 & 19) featuring the painting of King George IV arriving at Leith, 15th August 1822.

Lieutenant Colonel William P C McNair – for his editing of the information on Highland Regiments and their tartans for the chapter Uniforms for the Services (page 31).

Erskine Veterans Charity – for permission to use the photograph of Squadron Leader Colin McGregor (page 35) at the launch of the Erskine Veterans Tartan in Lossiemouth 2006.

Sir Jackie and Paul Stewart – for permission to include the photograph of the Stewart Grand Prix Team in The Heritage Story of Kinloch Anderson chapter (page 50).

Patrick Straub – for permission to include photographs of the Basel Tattoo tartan, event and officials in The Heritage Story of Kinloch Anderson chapter (page 50).

Brooks Brothers Limited – for permission to include the photographs of Kinloch Anderson at Brooks Brothers 1955 in the chapter Early Marketing, Exporting and Brand Development (page 90).

David Watt – for permission to include the photograph of the Institute of Directors tartan in the chapter The Global Impact of Tartan (page 102).

The Caledonian Club, London – for permission to include the photograph of The Caledonian Club tartan in the chapter The Global Impact of Tartan (page 103).

Professor Chris West – for permission to include photographs of the Edinburgh Zoo Panda Tartan in the chapter The Global Impact of Tartan (page 103).

The Drambuie Liqueur Company – for permission to include the photograph of the Drambuie tartan in the chapter The Global Impact of Tartan (page 103)

George Mackenzie – for his editing of information on the Scottish Register of Tartans (page 112) in the chapter The Global Impact of Tartan.

Keith Walker – for permission to include the photograph of Highland Dancers at the Royal Edinburgh Military Tattoo (page 114) in the chapter The Global Impact of Tartan

The Renaissance Golf Club, East Lothian – for permission to include the photograph of The Renaissance Club tartan carpet in The Global Impact of Tartan chapter (page 114).

Neil Paton – for permission to include the photograph of the Old Course Hotel St Andrews tartan merchandise (page 114) in the chapter The Global Impact of Tartan.

The City of Edinburgh Council – for permission to include the photograph of the crew of the Edinburgh Inspiring Capital yacht in the Clipper Round the World Yacht Race (page 115) in the chapter The Global Impact of Tartan.

Steve Lindridge – for permission to include the photograph of Team Scotland at the Melbourne Opening Ceremony 2006 (page 115) in the chapter The Global Impact of Tartan.

Jim Potter of Elevation Design – for permission to reproduce photographs of The Kinloch Anderson Heritage Room, and The Heritage Room panels, in The Kinloch Anderson Heritage Room chapter (page 119).

Lynne Morris – for permission to include the panoramic photograph of the Kinloch Anderson Shop (pages 158 & 159).

Harry Griffiths, photographer – for his work on Highland Dress photographs 1999 and 2002.

Paul Marr, photographer – for his work on Highland Dress and Scottish Dress For Ladies photographs 2009.

Amanda Noble, Sally Smith and Kirsty Franey – Kinloch Anderson members of staff, for assistance in the creation of this book.